rescues!

• • •

true stories from the edge

Look for more exciting titles in the award-winning series
True Stories from the Edge:

Thieves! by Andreas Schroeder

Of all the crimes people commit, stealing is the most common. These stories of incredible heists take readers into the realm of serious criminals, from the notorious to the strangely heart-warming.

Scams! by Andreas Schroeder

Scam artists have been tricking people for a very long time. These dramatic stories explore some of the most outrageous and inventive swindlers of all time.

Fires! by Tanya Lloyd Kyi

Step into the blinding flames, the choking smoke, and the waves of heat that brought humans face-to-face with one of the world's mightiest natural forces.

Tunnels! by Diane Swanson

People have been tunneling since the Stone Age. These gripping stories of human drama beneath the ground are fast-paced and tension-filled.

Escapes! by Laura Scandiffio

History is full of daring escapes. The exhilarating stories in this collection take readers around the world and across the ages.

Tanya Lloyd Kyi

rescues!

**Ten dramatic stories
of life-saving heroics**

annick press
toronto + new york + vancouver

Annick Press Ltd.

We acknowledge the support of the Canada Council for the Arts, the Ontario Arts
Council, and the Government of Canada through the Book Publishing Industry
Development Program (BPIDP) for our publishing activities.

Edited by Pam Robertson
Copy-edited by Elizabeth McLean
Proofread by Helen Godolphin and Melissa Edwards
Cover and interior design by Irvin Cheung and Amy Lau/iCheung Design
Cover illustration by Scott Cameron

Cataloging in Publication
Lloyd Kyi, Tanya 1973-
     Rescues! / written by Tanya Lloyd Kyi.

(True stories from the edge)
Includes bibliographical references and index.
ISBN-13: 978-1-55451-034-4 (bound)
ISBN-10: 1-55451-034-1 (bound)
ISBN-13: 978-1-55451-033-7 (pbk.)
ISBN-10: 1-55451-033-3 (pbk.)

1. Rescues Juvenile literature. I. Title. II. Series.

HV553.K95 2006   j904   C2006-901159-1

Printed and bound in Canada

Published in the U.S.A. by	Distributed in Canada by	Distributed in the U.S.A. by
Annick Press (U.S.) Ltd.	Firefly Books Ltd.	Firefly Books (U.S.) Inc.
	66 Leek Crescent	P.O. Box 1338
	Richmond Hill, ON	Ellicott Station
	L4B 1H1	Buffalo, NY 14205

Visit our website at **www.annickpress.com**

Contents

Introduction

Putting Life on the Line

In October 1995, Hurricane Roxanne whipped the Gulf of Mexico into a chaos of four-story waves. Caught in the storm and blasted by winds howling at 140 kilometres (90 miles) per hour were 245 workers on board Derrick Lay Barge 269. And the barge was sinking.

Longer than a football field and used to lay underwater pipelines between oil rigs and the shores of Mexico, the massive barge was more than 20 years old. It had been battered by too many storms, and with its rusty seams and outdated equipment, was no longer capable of riding hurricane waters. Within a few hours after the storm struck, the equipment rooms were filling with water. When the force of the waves snapped the towlines between the barge and the two tugboats responsible for pulling it through the water, the barge was left without power and with little ability to float. It slowly settled deeper and deeper into the ocean until the waves crashed over every surface of the deck.

One by one, most of the 245 workers jumped from the barge into the sea, to be picked up by the waves and slammed underwater. It was like being lifted to the top of a cliff, then dropped to the bottom, again and again. Many of the inflatable life rafts were picked up like cardboard and blown away by the wind.

Mexico has no coast guard, and boats from the navy and the U.S. Coast Guard were too far away to help. The workers' only hope lay in the captains of the two tugboats who had been pulling the barge, and the crew of one other tugboat that happened to be in the area.

It was growing dark. Pitching onto the crests of waves, then hurtling into the troughs, the three tugboats struggled to get near the floating workers without crushing them under the bows of their boats. On board the *Captain John*, the smallest of the rescue boats, the crew tried roping themselves together for safety before they threw rescue lines to the survivors bobbing in the waves. By the time they had pulled a few men on board, their rescue lines were hopelessly tangled. They were forced to cut them off. After that, whenever a wave crashed across the boat, one man would yell and all crew members would drop to the deck, frantically grabbing any piece of equipment that would keep them from being swept into the sea. It became a rhythm: throw a rescue line, haul a survivor on board, drop as a wave tried to crush the boat, wait for the water to drain away, and toss another rescue line. One of the crew members was caught by a wave, battered against the deckhouse, then crushed against the bulwarks. Just as he was being swept over the edge of the stern, he managed to grab a pipe and stop his fall.

On the *Ducker Tide*, the supply tug that had responded to the barge's rescue signals, First Mate Hayman Webster scanned the water for the blinking emergency lights attached to each worker's life preserver. Hayman was a massive man and a second-generation sailor. As the captain brought the side of the boat crashing down toward swimming workers, Hayman would lean over the side, grab a life preserver in one enormous fist, and single-handedly heave a man onto the deck of his boat. He pulled dozens to safety before some of the rescued workers organized ropes and began hauling their fellow survivors on board.

On board the third tugboat, the *North Carolina*, the crew

huddled on the most sheltered sections of the deck, terrified of being swept off the rolling, lunging vessel. But First Mate Eulalio Zapata Martinez put the lives of the barge workers above his own safety. Seeing that other crew members were too frightened to help, Eulalio tied himself to a winch on deck and began leaning far over the side to haul survivors on board one by one.

Working alone, he was in constant danger of being swept overboard. The first time it happened, he dangled in midair, held by his safety line, until he could haul himself back. The second time, he caught hold of a cargo net and climbed to the deck. The third time, a wave slammed him into the hull, then buried him in water. Every time he tried to pull himself up, another swell crushed him. Finally, a wave spun him in the right direction and he grabbed the rails for long enough to save himself. And, eventually, a few of the rescued crew recovered enough to replace Eulalio at his work.

Throughout the evening, on all three boats, men labored to find and rescue the workers. By the time help reached them, some swimmers were too exhausted to hold onto a safety line. Others were covered with slippery oil and almost impossible to grab. Still others were injured or unconscious. For more than six hours, as the captains struggled to maneuver their tugs in impossible seas, the rescuers worked unceasingly. When the barge's crew could finally be gathered and tallied the following morning, all but 23 had been rescued. Fifteen more were found two days later, alive and tied to a part of the barge's crane equipment that had miraculously stayed above water. Only eight men were lost.

Before the Days of 911

Some rescue teams, like the tugboat crews of Hurricane Roxanne, are born amidst the chaos of a dangerous situation. People see a sudden need and band together to offer help. But throughout history, people have also worked to form more stable and permanent rescue and lifesaving groups.

As early as 24 B.C., the city of Rome founded a brigade of paid and trained firefighters to protect its citizens. In 1049, a group of monks built a hospice for travelers high in the Alps between Switzerland and Italy, and began to find and care for those who strayed from the dangerous mountain paths. In fact, it was these monks who bred and trained the first St. Bernard rescue dogs in the 1600s.

In North America, the first coastal rescue organization was founded in Massachusetts in the 1700s, intended to help sailors who were caught by the area's unpredictable weather or shipwrecked on the treacherous offshore sandbars. In the early 1800s, the government ordered navy boats to patrol the coast during the annual storm season and rescue vessels in trouble—a precursor to today's coast guards.

The innovations of the 19th century brought the need for new kinds of lifesaving. An increase in swimming pools and swimming competitions had led to more drowning deaths, and in 1892 British swimming champion William Henry helped to form a society that taught rescue and first aid skills to expert swimmers—the first lifeguards. The same society now has branches in 50 countries.

There's also a third type of rescue team—not as official as a coast guard, yet not as spontaneous as the Hurricane Roxanne crews. Sometimes people have cooperated with their friends or neighbors to act against injustices in the world around them. For example, in the late 1700s and early 1800s, farmers, business owners, and other citizens of the United States and Canada formed the Underground Railroad to help lead escaped slaves to freedom. Each operator on the "railroad" knew of a few other operators or safe houses nearby, but didn't know the details of the full operation. That way, one captured operator couldn't destroy the entire route.

The Underground Railroad is only one story of ordinary people who saw a problem and unofficially banded together to solve it. A century later, other groups formed to help Jews flee persecution and death during World War II. And in France, an entire town took action.

Le Chambon-sur-Lignon

In the late 1930s, high in the mountains of southern France, Pastor Daniel Trocmé was enjoying the warmth of his home as the winter weather swirled around the village of Le Chambon-sur-Lignon. Suddenly, he heard a knock at the door. Pastor Trocmé wasn't expecting anyone, but it wasn't uncommon for a parishioner to arrive late at night seeking care or advice.

He opened the door—and found not a parishioner, but a woman he'd never seen before. She was shivering in the cold. She was a Jew, she said. Could she come in?

Pastor Trocmé knew the German army was quickly overwhelming the French forces. (In fact, France would soon surrender to Germany and establish a new, German-friendly government.) All Jewish people were to be turned over to German authorities, and anyone sheltering a Jew could be arrested.

Despite knowing this, Pastor Trocmé opened his door. And that Sunday, he began talking to his congregation about compassion, peace, and pacifism. Although his teachings became so dangerous that even a national church leader asked him to stop, Pastor Trocmé kept preaching. And his congregation kept listening.

Slowly, they began to shelter more and more Jewish refugees

in their homes. When army officers began asking questions, the villagers prepared a series of hiding places in basements, in barns, or in the nearby woods. They were able to whisk the refugees to safety when police raided the village. Once the officers were gone, villagers would walk through the woods singing a certain song to let all those in hiding know it was once again safe to go inside. Sometimes villagers sheltered the same refugees for several years. But often, they were able to arrange ways to help people reach the safety of the Swiss border.

The raids became more threatening, yet the residents of Le Chambon were always innocently working or sleeping when the police arrived. Their secret was the cooperation of some police force members, who had also heard and been influenced by Pastor Trocmé's messages. Even when German soldiers arrived in 1942, villagers continued their rescue operations. They always seemed to receive advance warning of raids on the area.

As the rescue efforts continued, Pastor Trocmé's cousin was sent to a concentration camp and killed. Pastor Trocmé himself was arrested. He was eventually released, but forced to hide from the Nazis. His wife and the rest of the community continued his work while he was gone. By the end of the war, they had saved over 5000 Jews from imprisonment and death.

The Scale of Heroism

Like the men who rescued workers from the waves during Hurricane Roxanne, the people of Le Chambon braved a dangerous situation to help complete strangers. Often, whether rescuers are leaning over the edge of a boat and into crashing ocean waves, or building secret rooms in their attics or basements, they know that they are risking their own lives.

When they are interviewed, heroes often tell reporters that

they didn't stop to think—they saw people in trouble and leaped into action. They responded as if a fire had started and they were the firefighters on duty.

Most of us find it hard to imagine being in the middle of such an emergency. But what if the situation involved our own homes, or our own families? In that kind of dangerous situation—perhaps a house fire or a car accident—we might risk our lives to save our family members or our closest friends. And everyone has heard stories about mothers finding the incredible ability to lift cars and save their trapped children. Some of them are merely urban legends, but other cases have been witnessed and documented. Obviously, we can find amazing strength if it will help save the people we love.

Thai history celebrates the story of a queen who went to extraordinary lengths to protect her husband. Queen Suriyothai lived in the 1500s. When she heard her husband was going to war against the Burmese, Suriyothai disguised herself as a man and rode as a warrior with her husband's army. Eventually, the Thai king and the Burmese king faced each other in battle, both mounted on their war elephants. The Burmese king raised his spear. Seeing her husband in danger, Suriyothai drove her own elephant in front of his. She was immediately killed.

Shamed by the queen's death, the Burmese king withdrew his army, and the Thai king returned home alive and victorious, saved by his wife's brave deed.

Suriyothai's sacrifice was an amazing display of love and dedication. But whether an emergency happens on a battlefield or on a mountain peak, most of us can't hope for a disguised warrior queen to suddenly reveal herself. And we can't wait for our mothers to show superhuman strength. If we're in a car accident, or caught in a storm, or struck by an avalanche, we must rely on the skill and dedication of strangers to rescue us. On the streets of our modern cities, those heroes might be paramedics or police officers. But in the newly settled Australian outback, people found heroism in a more unlikely source…

The Legend of Yarri

In the mid-1800s, deep in the Australian desert, merchants founded a town at a river crossing where travelers needed to stop and restock. Year after year, the local Aboriginal people warned the settlers that their town of Gundagai was in danger—the river could flood and destroy everything along its banks. Still, despite the warnings and despite some springtime floods, the town continued to grow. Not only were the Aboriginal people ignored, they were treated with scorn and disdain by many of the white settlers.

In June 1852, it rained constantly for three weeks. On the morning of Thursday, June 24, the water poured over the banks of the river, through the streets, and into people's homes. Then it rose, first through the bottom stories, then through the second stories, until the settlers were forced onto rooftops and surrounded by a raging tide of mud- and debris-choked water. At least 80 people drowned, their bodies swept away by the flood. A rowboat that was usually used to ferry people across the river was caught by the current and smashed against a tree, leaving no way to save the survivors. By Friday, the water was rising up to a meter (3 feet) each hour, and the people trapped on rooftops were suffering from hypothermia and shock.

Paddling by himself in a bark canoe, an Aboriginal man named Yarri braved the flood waters. Kneeling in the base of his vessel, he maneuvered across the current with a single paddle until he could reach a survivor—one passenger was all his boat would carry. Having scooped someone up, he would negotiate back across the current to safety. Throughout the day, Yarri made the trip again and again. When it grew dark, he had to search for survivors by following their shouts and cries.

On Saturday, another Aboriginal man named Jacky Jack arrived to help, with a canoe that could hold several people at once. Together, Yarri and Jacky Jack worked throughout the next day, the following night, and a third day. The two men saved a total of 69 people, despite the fact that the white settlers had treated them badly, and despite the fact that the settlers had been repeatedly warned of the danger.

Today, the town of Gundagai (rebuilt in a location less vulnerable to floods) is still home to the descendants of people rescued by Yarri and Jacky Jack more than 150 years ago.

IT SEEMS THAT IN DANGEROUS SITUATIONS, the ties that bind humans together as a common species are stronger than the difficulties of nationality or race. Fortunately for those in need, rescuers often don't stop to ask whether rappelling down the face of a mountain, hanging from a helicopter, or paddling into floodwaters is safe or reasonable. In fact, we call rescuers "heroes" for exactly that reason—because they don't weigh their own lives against those of others.

The rescuers in the stories that follow ran through landslides, dangled over cliffs, and dove to the ocean floor all for the sake of strangers. In one story, more than 50 men climbed a treacherous mountain face to rescue stranded climbers, even though they didn't know who the climbers were or even what language they spoke. In another, men from seven countries traveled by ship, plane, and dogsled into the Arctic because they had heard an explorer was in danger.

Every hero in every one of these stories risked his or her life to bring people back from the very edge of death. They proved that even during disasters or horrible tragedies, people can achieve amazing good.

Death on the North Face

The Eiger, Switzerland, August 1957

GÜNTHER NOTHDURFT STOOD AT THE BASE of the Eiger, gazing up at the soaring rock face above him. It was one of the deadliest climbs in Europe.

He shook his hands and reached for the first holds on the rock, ready to begin his reconnaissance mission. He would scout the routes, climb the first few cliffs, and return later if he wanted to tackle the entire face. Although he was only 22, Günther wasn't an impulsive mountaineer. He planned every trip, trained for weeks before his major climbs, and made notes of each success and each mistake. His combination of natural talent and careful plotting had made him one of the best young climbers in the world. Already, he had conquered some of Europe's most difficult routes.

Usually, climbs like the north face of the Eiger are done in teams of two. The first climber wedges and pounds metal pitons into the rock and fastens them to a rope. The second climber follows the route of the first, relying on the same rope and removing the equipment as he climbs. Theoretically, if one climber falls, the pitons will hold to the rock, allowing the second climber to grip the rope and stop the fall. In reality, the force of a fall will sometimes pull the pitons free, sending both climbers careening down the mountain.

Günther's method of climbing the Eiger was even more

dangerous. He was by himself, relying only on his own pitons and ice ax to hold him. This sort of solo-climbing was part of what had made Günther famous in mountaineering circles. He had already soloed a hazardous climb in Italy called the Yellow Arête. He was only the second man to succeed, and he did the climb in an hour less than the first man.

On the lower pitches of the Eiger, Günther climbed steadily, with unwavering confidence. A fellow climber had once said that Günther had only one speed—full steam ahead. He powered through the first parts of the mountain: the Difficult Crack, the Hinterstoisser Traverse, the First Ice Field, and the route toward the Second. It was going so well that he began to think his reconnaissance mission might actually turn out to be a *solo* climb of the Eiger, something that had never been done before.

At the base of the Second Ice Field, he bivouacked (or camped) on a ledge for some rest, attached to the side of the mountain with pitons and rope. At 3 a.m., after a few hours of sleep, he was about to continue the climb. He lifted his water bottle to his lips for one last sip.

Smash!

Günther was suddenly holding shards of glass. A rock had tumbled down the mountain face and shattered his bottle, missing his head by a breath. He had discovered one of the main dangers of the Eiger—loose rock was held in place only by ice and snow. A mere shift of the wind could send a shower of boulders onto climbers below.

The near brush with death sent Günther backtracking down the mountain, no longer so confident. Back in Munich, he mentioned the climb to the owner of a sports shop:

"I have been to the Eiger north wall," he said, "and there is death in it."

The Ogre

Günther wasn't exaggerating. There was plenty of death on the north face of the Eiger. Prone to avalanches and rockslides, beaten by thunderstorms and blizzards, and covered in crumbling rock and deadly ice, the 3970-meter (13,000-foot) peak was a mountaineer's worst nightmare. In fact, by 1957 the face had been successfully climbed only 12 times, and 15 climbers had fallen to their deaths. The famous Sherpa guide Tenzing Norgay, one of the first men to conquer Everest, tried the Eiger and proclaimed it too difficult and too dangerous. Even its name— "the ogre" in German—was a warning.

The local Swiss guides who were responsible for plucking stranded mountaineers off the Bernese Alps believed the Eiger was so hazardous that no one should climb it. There were some cliff faces in the world that were too dangerous ever to be climbed by humans, and with unstable rock and unpredictable weather, the Eiger was one of them. Too many people had already died. Why should the guides have to risk their lives saving climbers who seemed determined to kill themselves?

None of this stopped two Italians, Claudio Corti and Stefano Longhi, from spending the spring and summer of 1957 planning for an ascent. They wanted their attempt to be a secret, imagining the astonishment that would greet them when they conquered the peak. Every weekend, they met or they climbed separately, training their bodies.

A wiry 29-year-old truck driver, Claudio was experienced but impulsive. Scorning maps and guides, he preferred to conquer routes by trial and error and he had relied on his instincts and strength to pull him through some extremely challenging climbs. But among the European climbing community, his reputation for daring was overshadowed by rumors about his frighteningly bad luck. Once, a bolt of lightning had sliced his climbing rope in two, sending Claudio's partner hurtling to his death.

Stefano was a 44-year-old factory worker who weighed over 90 kilograms (200 pounds). He climbed regularly, but he had never done any of Europe's most challenging peaks. Still, he loved the thrill of the sport and he admired the more experienced Claudio. With his friend's encouragement, he was eager to challenge the Eiger.

Following their plan of secrecy, the pair quietly began their ascent on the morning of August 3. They wore the bright red jackets of their Italian climbing club and they carried tea, coffee, sugar, ham, biscuits, and dried fruit to last four days, a small stove and fuel, medicine, a small bottle of cognac, rope, carabiners (metal clips to attach to the rope), rock pitons, ice pitons, crampons (to help their boots stick to the ice), sleeping bags, and ice axes. Unfortunately, the pair chose the wrong approach route and wasted the entire first day. They camped on the rock, then retraced their steps early the next morning until they found the proper course. At last, they were scaling the face of the Eiger.

No one had successfully climbed the face for four years. So imagine their surprise when, halfway through their breakfast on Monday, August 5, they saw two other climbers moving toward them.

It was Günther Nothdurft, back for a second attempt. This time, the young German was climbing with a partner, Franz Mayer. The two men had planned a two-week climbing vacation in the Alps and at the last minute Günther had received a telegram from a friend:

CONDITIONS BERNESE OBERLAND EXCELLENT.

Both Günther and Franz knew immediately what that meant: it was cold and crisp enough to freeze the rocks of the Eiger in place. If they snatched the opportunity, they could climb the north face.

After an excited conversation, the two men decided to take up the challenge. Casting aside his usual painstaking planning, Günther bought a postcard-sized map of the climbing route, packed his gear, and began confidently leading Franz up the face. After all, he'd already successfully climbed the first part of the route on his earlier trip.

When they met that morning, the Italians and the Germans introduced themselves, had some simple sign-language conversations, then continued climbing on their two separate ropes. They camped that night on ledges near each other.

In the morning, Günther and Franz discovered that their food bag had fallen off the ledge. Once they understood the problem through signs and simple words, the Italians were nice enough to share their breakfast, and the four men continued the climb, confident they would reach the top before hunger hampered them.

But now, on the fourth day of the climb, the pace suddenly slowed. Of the Italians, the less experienced Stefano was tired, both physically and mentally. They were 1200 meters (4000 feet), then 1500 meters (5000 feet) above the valley, and gazing so far down every day was beginning to play tricks with his mind. He lost some of his confidence and spent extra minutes enlarging each toe hold. Meanwhile, on the German rope, Günther was suffering from stomach cramps and a gripping headache. He, too, plodded along. By the end of the day, the climbers were only at the top of the Second Ice Field, about halfway up the mountain.

Günther felt better on Wednesday, which was day five, but his stomach cramps returned partway through the morning, leaving him pale and clinging to the rock. On the Italian team, Stefano was completely worn out. They spent the night perched on the mountain in freezing rain.

In hindsight, many climbers say that the two teams should have turned back. They were ridiculously short of food and they were exhausted. But at the time, Claudio believed that the climb down would be just as difficult as the climb up. Once they reached the top, it was a comparatively easy hike to the tourist railway that could take them safely back to the valley, down a less steep side of the mountain.

So on day six, all four climbers clipped into the same rope, allowing Claudio to lead while Franz and Günther took the easier, safer positions in the middle. Stefano was the anchor, responsible for removing the equipment from the rock and holding the rope if anyone fell. They continued, climb after climb. Waterfall Crack. The Ice Bulge. The Ramp Snowfield. The Traverse of the Gods. At one point, Claudio misjudged a route, costing the team valuable time. Still, they moved on, almost to the edge of the Spider Snowfield, three-quarters of the way to the peak.

Disaster

"Falling! Hold me!"

Suddenly Stefano's shout echoed across the rock and the rope went slipping through Claudio's hands. As he tightened his grip, the friction sent smoke spiraling from his climbing gloves. In a fraction of a second, the rope had burned through the gloves and into his hands. Desperately, he ground his teeth and hung on, bracing his legs against the ledge. Somehow he stopped the rope. Stefano swung in the air, hidden from sight by an overhang below.

Shouting instructions back and forth, the men managed to lower Stefano one more body length to a ledge, where he stood stranded. His hands were frozen, his mind numb, and he was unable to pull himself up. Claudio tried to single-handedly pull his friend to safety, but the weight of the big man was too much for him. The German pair were clinging in insecure places to the rock, unable to help because of the angles of the rope.

After three hours of hauling on the rope with his burned hands, Claudio gave up. He lowered a little food and water to the ledge below and called encouraging words to Stefano. The remaining three would press on to the summit and send for help.

Through the Lens

Almost every day, Fritz von Almen peered through the lenses of the telescopes at his hotel, across the valley from the Eiger. The face had made him famous, both with the climbers who used his hotel as a base and with the tourists who came to watch the action.

But as Fritz watched the climbers crawl their way up the mountain, he found it increasingly difficult to turn away. Again and again, a voice inside his head said they weren't going to make it. They were moving so slowly that something had to be wrong.

Fritz already knew that the local rescue squad would do nothing to help. The climbers were too far up for a simple rescue from the base, and too far down to make a rescue from the summit easy. Besides, the position of the Bernese rescuers was clear: those who climbed the Eiger did so at their own risk.

There must be someone who could help. As Fritz pressed his eye to the telescope once again, he thought of a Swiss mountaineer who had stopped by the day before. Robert Seiler had climbed the Eiger himself and knew its dangers. More importantly, he knew a network of mountaineering experts that extended across Europe.

Shaking his head, Fritz put through a call to Robert. The climbers were in trouble, he explained, and there was no one else to help.

Robert spent the next six hours on the phone, interrupting climbers at their workplaces, tracking them down on their summer vacations, and asking German and Austrian climbing clubs for help.

Less than two days later, he was leading seven men up the mountain into an unpredictable rescue. Two of the climbers were known—the German pair. But who were the men in the bright red jackets?

To Robert, it didn't matter. Whoever they were, they needed help.

AROUND THE SAME TIME, others began to notice the strange set of climbers or hear rumors about an unfolding tragedy. Soon, expert mountaineers who happened to be climbing in the area began to turn up at the base of the Eiger and volunteer their skills. A famous French mountain guide and his clients offered to help, as did a Swiss rescue team, and one of Günther's experienced climbing friends.

Fifty-one-year-old German rescue expert Ludwig Gramminger was shaving when he heard a radio report about the crisis. With his face half-slathered in shaving cream, he began calling the members of his team, the Munich Mountain Guard of the German Red Cross. Ludwig had invented a list of rescue equipment that ranged from winch and cable systems for lifting climbers to a backpack-style harness for carrying injured men to safety. When others shook their heads and said situations were hopeless, Ludwig and his friend Alfred Hellepart went into action.

Bad weather prevented Ludwig and Alfred from flying into Switzerland, but they loaded their equipment and teammates into Ludwig's Volkswagen and started driving toward the wall, determined to launch a rescue.

Another Man Down

Meanwhile, the situation on the mountain had grown worse. Claudio, Günther, and Franz had spent Friday afternoon struggling slowly up the field of ice and snow known as the White Spider. Günther spent agonizing periods bent double with stomach pains, but the men had conquered the most difficult part of the climb and were now about 210 meters (700 feet) from the peak.

Suddenly Claudio was falling, his body bashing against the mountain face as he tumbled. A rock had rolled down the cliff and knocked him on the head, pulling him off the face. For a long moment, he hung upside down, watching drops of blood fall from his scalp onto the snow below. Then with a jerk on the rope, he was upright. With the help of the Germans, he crawled back up.

When the climbers reunited, the German pair soon realized that Claudio was incoherent and unable to continue climbing. They held up their fingers, trying to make him understand that if he stayed where he was, safe on the ledge, they would return with help by five o'clock the next evening. Claudio climbed into his sleeping bag and promptly passed out.

Crawling to the Rescue

The early hours of Saturday morning found Robert Seiler leading a 29-man rescue squad as they inched their way across a traverse toward the peak. There was an easier approach, but bad weather the night before had made them choose the high route. At one point, one of the rescuers fell into a crevasse and it took several men to pull him out, bruised and shaking.

Two other men took the easier route up the west wall of the mountain and beat the main team to the summit. They began hacking a large flat platform out of the ice, a place to set up the pulley systems. Chilled and tired, they were nonetheless determined. On the way up the mountain, they had heard a voice calling out for help. The climber was too far away to reach, or even to see, but at least he was alive.

LUDWIG AND ALFRED of the Munich Mountain Guard had also collected more volunteers, including two well-known Italian climbers and eight Polish mountaineers. By mid-morning, their group was scaling the easier west wall route. Partway up, they also heard a weak voice echoing across the rock.

"Who are you?" called one of the Italians.

"Longhi! Stefano!"

Now, for the first time, the team knew who needed rescuing.

"We have come to save you," they called.

"Come to help," came Stefano's reply. "Hungry! Cold!"

ALL WAS NOT SMOOTH on the summit. Robert had failed to get most of his men over the traverse. Twenty-one had to turn back and try again up the west wall. Still, they could begin arranging the equipment. Three painstaking hours later, they were ready to lower a scout to find the stranded climbers.

Attached to the cable, Robert was slowly inched down the face. He found himself holding his breath, knowing any sudden movement could send rock and snow onto the trapped men below. For 120 meters (400 feet), he hung in the freezing wind, calling to the climbers. There was no response. When he was finally winched back to the peak, frostbite forced him to leave the mountain.

The rescuers repositioned the winch and at dusk another man was lowered. The cable wasn't in quite the right place—he couldn't reach the red tent where he believed three climbers were stranded. But this time, a voice called out from the ledge.

As the rescuer was pulled back to the peak, temperatures began to drop toward freezing.

BY NIGHTFALL, LUDWIG'S TEAM and Robert's team had merged on the summit. They were preparing to camp for the night—most without food or proper camping equipment—when a lone climber reached them. It was another friend of Günther's. There were now 50 men on the rescue crew.

Many of them had years of experience on some of the world's most treacherous mountains. Others had led multiple successful rescue missions. There could easily have been arguments over who should and would lead the next day's operations. It was also less than two decades after the close of World War II, and everyone on the rescue team was old enough to remember the bitterness of the war.

Yet on the mountain, climbers from once opposing countries like Germany, France, and Poland had been thrown together without any notion of nationality. Despite all their differences, the men found themselves eager to work together. They were all focused on one goal—to save the men on the face.

Into the Abyss

When they awoke chilled and stiff on Sunday morning, the ninth day, it was the Munich rescue expert, Ludwig, who took over the arrangement of the winch system. Another team worked on a backup plan, clearing a path to allow a line of men to hoist the cable if the winch failed.

The men knew that Stefano was alone on the lower ledge, and hoped the other three climbers were together in the red tent on a higher outcrop of rock. Their plan was to lower a rescuer to Stefano, haul him up to the red tent, then lower rescuers one at a time to retrieve all four climbers.

Alfred, who knew the intricacies of his friend Ludwig's winch system, would make the first descent. Though he had absolute trust in his friend, Alfred still felt moments of panic as they lowered him over the side. At times he hung helpless while the ground spun so far below him that misty clouds hid it. He tested his radio connection and heard the calm voices of his colleagues above.

Finally, after what seemed like an endless trip down, he was able to grasp the wall and begin climbing across the cliff. He spotted a man sitting on the outcrop with the red tent, but he couldn't tell who it was. Then, with a surge of frustration, Alfred realized he wasn't going to be able to reach the climber. The cable was too far to one side. Even if he climbed over to the man, the crew on top wouldn't be able to pull them up without sending them wildly swinging into the face.

Communicating constantly by radio, Alfred had the summit team haul him higher on the cliff—a pull that seemed a short distance on the Eiger, but was actually the height of a 15-story building. Then he began slowly to pick his way back down by another route, trying to get closer to the outcrop. As he stepped and slid, he yelled for the stranded climber to take cover—cascades of loose rocks showered down beneath his feet. Finally, he was on the outcrop with the red tent. He found the climber lucid, but shaking with hunger and cold, his teeth chipped from gnawing at the ice on the ledge.

But there was only one man—Claudio. Where were the other two? Alfred was appalled to discover that the two Germans had continued climbing and had somehow disappeared.

At the summit, meanwhile, the rescuers had a decision to make. Would they rescue Claudio now, or leave him on the ledge and go lower for Stefano? Claudio was in bad condition, and the short period of hauling Alfred higher on the rope had been tough on the equipment. They decided to take Claudio first.

As Alfred helped the man into the backpack-like harness, the crew at the top dealt with another problem. The winch wasn't going to be strong enough to lift both men. The rescuers prepared to pull the climbers to the summit by hauling in the rope by hand. Now they needed every bit of strength they had, and every person on the gigantic rescue team. Hand over hand, their arms straining at the rope and their feet braced in the snow, they pulled, in a deadly tug-of-war against the Eiger.

For forty minutes, with the weight of Claudio shifting on his back and the weight of the radio pressing into his chest, Alfred hung on the cable. He clung to ledges where he could; at other times he spun helplessly in midair. At last, with one great heave, the team hauled them onto the summit.

Claudio was alive.

HE WOULD BE THE ONLY ONE of the four climbers to survive the Eiger ascent. Although the rescuers tried to return for Stefano that night, lowering a French guide down the cable, poor radio communications and an incoming storm forced them to delay. Half the team then made the trek down the west wall of the mountain, lowering Claudio in a stretcher. It took them two days in the midst of a lightning storm to carry the sometimes delirious climber to safety.

Still hoping to save Stefano, the other half of the team stood by at the summit. Tragically, a plane the next morning spotted Stefano's rigid, frozen body dangling from the ropes; the wind had pulled him from the ledge during the night. His body hung there, visible through the telescopes across the valley, for two years until a rescue squad was able to reach it.

Deadly Rumors

But what had happened to the pair of German climbers, Günther and Franz? Once Claudio was recovering from his frostbite and shock, journalists and even police investigators questioned him again and again. About other parts of the climb, he was unsure. But he clearly remembered Günther and Franz holding up five fingers. They had pressed on toward the summit, and had promised to return at 5 p.m. the next day.

When searchers could find no signs of the Germans, rumors spread that Claudio had sabotaged the others so that he could keep their food and drink for himself. There was absolutely no evidence to support the rumor, but Claudio lived under a constant cloud of suspicion. It wasn't until 1961 that his name was cleared. Climbers stumbled upon two bodies curled up together near the summit and linked by a climbing rope.

It was Günther and Franz. They were only a short distance from where the 50-man rescue squad would have been working in 1957, and less than an hour from the safety of the mountain train station. Having reached the summit and conquered the Eiger, they had been caught in an avalanche or wandered off course in the dark, and had frozen to death on the mountain's slope.

They were the 17th and 18th victims of the Eiger's north face.

The Mountain That Walked

Frank, Canada, April 29, 1903

ENGINEER BEN MURGATROYD eased the freight train engine
along the track, pulling several boxcars of coal away from the
mine. It was 4 a.m., but the frigid air and the strain of the job kept
him wide awake. He'd already guided the train through a snow-
storm that night, and he'd spent the rest of the journey through
the Crowsnest Pass constantly scanning the dark tracks for broken
rails or boulders. The route through the Rocky Mountains to
Turtle Mountain and the town of Frank was always treacherous.
And at the end of the long journey, already tired, Ben had guided
the train up the long inclines and onto the mountain itself. He
was ready to return to the station and enjoy a long rest.

An echoing crack penetrated the bellow of the train's engine,
and Ben caught a sudden movement from the corner of his eye.
He looked up to see a massive boulder tumbling from the side of
the mountain, bouncing from the rock faces and rolling between
trees as if it were a child's toy. Another was rolling close behind.

Shouting to his small crew, Ben released the brakes on the
engine and let the train loose on the downward slope. The men
inside leaped for handholds. Outside, brakemen Sid Choquette
and Bill Lowes had been running alongside the engine. They
dove for the sides of the train and fought to hold on, praying for
their lives.

With an explosive roar, the mountain seemed to split in half and a tidal wave of rock swept toward the tracks. Ben braced himself and focused on the wooden bridge ahead. If they could just clear the river…

As boulders thundered down the slope, time seemed to slow. Ben leaned forward, as if urging the train ahead with his body. He focused only on the bridge, never looking back, but he could hear the destruction behind him as the slide ripped through the tracks where the train had stood seconds before. Sparks flew as boulder hit boulder in midair.

Just to the bridge, Ben thought. Just to the bridge.

Then, at last, the engine was on the span, with Sid and Bill still clinging to the outside. In a heartbeat, the train had careened onto the opposite slope. Behind it, rocks smashed into the bridge, splintering logs as if they were toothpicks and sending the structure flying into the river below.

When Ben finally caught his breath, the roaring had stopped, replaced by an eerie silence. The mountain behind him was gone.

In the darkness, Ben couldn't see the extent of the disaster. He would later discover that in less than two minutes, 30 million cubic meters (1 billion cubic feet) of rock had swept down the mountain—so much debris that 4 million dump trucks would have been needed to move it. Of course, many of the boulders that fell were much larger than dump trucks. Some were the size of small apartment buildings.

The slide had raced down the mountain so fast that it had spread across 9 square kilometers (3.5 square miles) of the valley and up the opposite mountain slopes, damming a river and burying the highway, the railroad tracks, and the eastern section of Frank, a town at the edge of what is now Alberta. At the time, Frank was home to about 600 people, most of them railway workers, mine workers, and their families. About 100 of the residents lived in the direct path of the slide.

Strangely enough, Ben and his crew had actually been lucky that they were on the mountain itself. If the train had been delayed, they might still have been on the railway tracks that entered the valley from the east—tracks now buried under rock.

Stop That Train!

The train's crew gathered at the station on the undamaged side of town, out of the path of danger. They were still reeling from the events of the last few minutes. Suddenly, Sid Choquette and Bill Lowes threw down their drinks and raced outside. The small group of remaining crew members raised their eyebrows at each other. Had the strain been two much? Had the two men suddenly gone insane?

Sid and Bill were already too far away to care what their fellow workers thought. They had remembered that the passenger train *Spokane Flyer* was due in Frank at 4:30 a.m. In the dark, the engineer wouldn't be able to see the landslide in time to stop the train. If he wasn't warned, the passenger train would slam into a wall of rock. Sid and Bill had less than 20 minutes to cross the slide.

They ran through the dark with only handheld lanterns to guide them through the debris. Jagged rocks tore at their boots. Some of the boulders were still hot from the friction of the slide. And more rocks continued to cascade off the mountain above. After several minutes of dodging boulders and breathing the dust-choked air, with no end to the slide in sight, Bill gave up. Gasping, he motioned Sid to go on without him.

Sid barely paused. After awhile he lost track of time. Had he been running too long? Had the train already crashed? Surely he would have heard the collision.

Finally, he stumbled down the steep bank of the slide. Throughout a two-kilometer (1.2-mile) run, over unmarked debris, in complete darkness, he had somehow managed to hold a straight line. The railway tracks lay directly in front of him, and the train had not yet arrived.

He set off down the tracks. As soon as he heard the sound of the locomotive in the distance, he stood at the edge of the tracks and began waving his arms and holding his lantern in the air. Would they see him in time? He continued shouting and waving as the train bore down on him, the engine light blindingly bright in the darkness. Finally, he heard the squeal of brakes as the engineer slowed the train to a stop. The passengers aboard the *Spokane Flyer* were safe.

Buried Alive

Jessie Leitch was a teenager—the oldest of seven children—when her father moved their family from Manitoba to a small, newly built miner's cabin in Frank. Jessie's mother didn't like the new town. The peak of Turtle Mountain blocked out the sun by late afternoon and she said the shadows of the mountains closed her in. Still, she filled the home with piano music and books and potted flowers. Jessie and her brothers and sisters were happy clambering over the banks of the nearby river or following the stately North West Mounted Police officers as they patrolled the town on horseback.

One of Jessie's favorite neighbors was the Scottish minister, David Stewart. Wearing his kilt, David would sweep one of Jessie's small brothers onto his shoulders and lead all seven children on a ramble through the nearby hillsides, teaching them to identify the wildflowers there and telling them Scottish tales as they walked. To Jessie, the world seemed full of fun. At night, she curled up in her bed beside her sister Rosemary and dreamed of the next day's adventures.

On April 29, 1903, the roar of the slide jolted Jessie awake. She heard the groans of the cabin timbers moving and the crystal pings of breaking glass. Then suddenly she couldn't move. She couldn't breathe. She was pinned to her bed by a massive weight. Disoriented, Jessie tried to call to her sister but as soon as she opened her mouth, dust filled her throat. She managed to wiggle one hand free to block her face from the debris. The breeze brought a whisper of coal gas. Jessie closed her eyes and prayed for help.

It seemed like hours later that she heard footsteps. The boards and the iron headboard across her body pressed and shifted as people walked above. She tried to call out. Could they hear her? The pressure on her legs came and went as they walked to and fro. Then she heard shovels striking wood and metal. They were coming.

Jessie was in shock when someone finally lifted her from the wreckage. It was the minister, David Stewart. He and another local minister had led a rescue party to where the cabin had once stood. He held a sip of whiskey to Jessie's lips and she coughed and sputtered. The next thing she knew, she was in a neighbor's home, holding her younger sister as rescuers told them that their parents and their four brothers were dead. But their baby sister was safe. She had been thrown from the top of the house and landed on a bale of hay—a bale that had somehow traveled from the stables several blocks away.

As the minister was pulling Jessie and the other children from the rubble, Lucy Ennis searched desperately for her own child.

She had woken a few minutes before to the sound of rattling dishes.

"Don't worry," her husband Sam had said. "It's probably just an earthquake."

But before he finished his sentence, a noise like thunder enveloped them and they felt the house tilt and splinter around them. They were left pinned by the wreckage, trapped in the dark.

As her husband scrambled to get free, heaving timbers off them both and prying his legs from under the debris, Lucy used her one free arm to scrabble frantically through the mud for Gladys, her 15-month-old baby. Gladys had been sleeping right beside her. Was she dead? Was she dead? Fear pounded in Lucy like a heartbeat. Finally, her fingers brushed cloth. She grabbed it, dragging it closer.

It was Gladys, but she wasn't moving. Filled with dread, Lucy found Gladys's mouth in the dark and pried out a handful of mud. Finally, the baby began to wail. They were still trapped, but at least they were alive.

A Stranger to the Rescue

When the Union Hotel shook, traveler George Bond leaped from his bed and scrambled into his clothes, thinking there must have been an explosion at the mine. Darkness still hid the face of the mountain and the extent of the slide. In the valley, George could only make out a fire burning across Gold Creek. Carrying lanterns, he and a few other men raced toward it, only to find that the bridge had been pushed off its foundations by a wall of mud. Undaunted, George waded into the water. He was barely across when he heard cries for help.

What George and the other rescuers saw when they arrived

was too horrifying to think about. Cabins lay splintered, as if they had been built from straw. Massive boulders had plowed through homes. Dust rose in spirals from the debris, while here and there a few small fires burned.

George didn't know who he was helping, but he had arrived at the Ennis cabin. Sam had found his three older children shivering but unharmed, while Lucy was still trapped below the debris, clinging to baby Gladys. George and the other men set their lanterns to give them as much light as possible, and began to dig. It seemed achingly slow, scooping away clay and rocks with their bare hands, but finally Lucy was free. One arm dangled uselessly—her collarbone was broken.

When they heard cries from the back of the house, the rescuers rushed to aid Lucy's brother, James Warrington. As they lifted layers of boards and rock off him, James said he could feel something moving beneath his body. George and the other men carefully lifted James free and found the next-door-neighbor, Mrs. Watkins, struggling for breath underneath. They pulled her to safety just as the nearby timbers caught fire.

As soon as she was safe, George moved on, looking for survivors in the wreckage of another house, then another.

Perfect Timing

The residents who were safe in the undamaged buildings of Frank felt as if they had barely escaped death. Among them were people who should have been sleeping in the destroyed section of town. Only a whim the night before, or a chance encounter, or pure luck, had saved their lives.

Two of those who narrowly cheated death were Ellen Thornley and her brother John, a shoemaker. It was the last night of Ellen's visit to Frank. Early the next morning, she was planning to walk into town and catch the train back to her parents' home in Pincher Creek.

When the last customer left the shop, John surprised his sister with a suggestion. Why didn't they head into town, have some fun, and spend Ellen's last night at the hotel?

Ellen called the idea a silly whim, but John eventually won her over and the pair meandered their way into the village, talking to other young people along the way. They checked into the Frank Hotel, where every evening boasted a combination of drinks, cards, and gambling. And less than 12 hours later, their decision saved their lives. John's entire shop was buried in the rubble.

Around the time when Ellen and John were checking into the hotel, Lillian Clark dropped into bed exhausted. She had been working late at the boardinghouse every night. Usually, she staggered home in the dark after her shift was over. Tonight, for the first time, her mother had finally allowed Lillian to stay the night at the boardinghouse. It was the first time 15-year-old Lillian had ever stayed away from home.

Like everyone else in Frank, Lillian woke to what seemed like an earthquake. She hurried outside. No one seemed to know what had happened. A few men were calling for help and rushing into the darkness. Neighbors huddled close, their eyes wide. Dust filled the air. Slowly, Lillian began to understand. A landslide.

As soon as it was light enough to see, Lillian set off over the rocks toward her house. There was no trace of the cabin. Massive limestone slabs covered the area. Lillian was the only member of her family left alive.

Inside the Mine...

Miraculously, even though a section of the mountain had entirely disappeared, there were still men alive in the most unlikely place of all—inside the coal mine. Somehow the slide had thundered right overtop of their tunnels and caverns, leaving most of them trapped but unharmed.

The 19 men working the night shift were responsible more for maintenance than for mining. They repaired the tracks for the coal cars near the entrance, loaded the ore mined by the day shift, or inspected the timbers holding up the walls of the shaft. The jobs were lonely—men worked by themselves or in pairs, spread out from the entrance to the deepest tunnels, more than 1500 meters (5000 feet) within the mountain.

Alone in the rock, surrounded by darkness, to be hit by a blast of rushing air and slammed into the tunnel walls was terrifying. Thinking there must have been an explosion deep within the mine, they dropped their tools and raced for the entrance.

One by one, 17 men neared the entrance and saw the others gathered there. One was bleeding from a scalp wound; one was nursing a crushed leg. The others were gazing in shock at what had once been the tunnel opening. It was now a solid wall of rock. One of the men responsible for checking the rail tracks thought he recognized their position. He guessed that they were buried 90 meters (300 feet) deep.

A party set off to check the exit on the lower level, and found it flooded by the Old Man River, now dammed by the fallen rock outside. Other men checked the air shafts, and found them blocked as well. Struggling to stay calm, the miners looked at each other in silence. They were trapped underground, with the river rising to meet them and the air supply cut off. They wouldn't last long.

Inside the mine, the men collected their tools and set out to save themselves. Without success, they pried at the rocks and timbers blocking the main entrance. Changing tactics, they began to dig upward, through a seam of coal that was softer than the surrounding rock. Working in small shifts, they hacked away at the ore. No one was sure that they were close enough to the surface to succeed, but with the air supply dwindling they were determined to try. It was about 8 a.m.

ALMOST AS SOON AS THE FIRST SHOCK of the slide subsided, a party of miners had scrambled from the townsite onto the mountainside, searching for the mine entrance. They worked in the dark, in constant danger from the chunks of rock that continued to fall. When dawn broke, they had still found no sign of the tunnel. And instead of finding hope with the first rays of light, they instead saw the extent of the damage. The town's power plant, the stables, and the construction camp were entirely gone, along with many homes. Desperate, they launched a more organized rescue attempt. The mine engineer spread out the plans for the mine and attempted to landmark where the entrance *should* have been. Meanwhile, rescuers gathered timbers and strung ropes across the flooded river, allowing more men to join them on the mountainside.

In their heads, they heard the same voice saying "no one could still be alive in there," but they didn't say the words out loud. They all knew the men on the night shift. They knew their wives and their children. They were going to dig until they found them, or found their bodies.

Today, excavation equipment would power through such rubble, but the rescuers in Frank had only shovels, axes, and crowbars. As soon as the engineer pointed to the right spot, the workers began hacking at the slide and prying boulders away. A fan of men spread out above them, ready to warn the workers of any more falling rocks. They worked in 15-minute shifts, digging with all their might and then resting, again and again. They worked through breakfast, through lunch, and through the afternoon. They worked while the railroad organized a train to evacuate the town, and while reporters from across the country began rushing to the scene. They worked without pause for the entire day, but they barely made a dent in the rock.

BY AFTERNOON, the men inside the mine had also been digging for hours. Every drop of energy gone, they sat along the sides of the shaft holding their heads in their hands and thinking only of the families they would be leaving behind.

Only three men kept digging. They were still alive, they figured, so there was still hope.

Suddenly, Dan McKenzie's mining pick struck through the black rock and into open air. When he pulled it back, sunlight streamed through the hole. Immediately, men began to cheer. Those who had been exhausted a moment before felt themselves revive.

As the miners widened the hole, they found they couldn't escape from the shaft in that spot—too much rock and debris was still sliding past. But they could see an area a short distance away that looked hopeful. With new energy, they tunneled a second vertical shaft through another 11 meters (36 feet) of ore.

Thirteen hours after the slide, they emerged into daylight and saw, 45 meters (150 feet) below, the team of rescuers still digging at the mine entrance. Dan McKenzie shouted, and in a euphoric rush of cheering and crying, the two teams of diggers united on the mountainside.

A Fragile Balance

The Kootenay and Blackfoot native people who hunted in the Crowsnest Pass called Turtle Mountain "the mountain that walked" and refused to camp in its shadow, wary of the landslides and the occasional tremors that rocked its slopes. The miners had always ignored the stories, reassuring themselves that the slides had always been small. After all, the tremors within the mountain actually loosened the coal, making their jobs easier.

But after 1903, residents wondered if the remains of Frank were still in danger. It had been a terrible disaster: more than 70 people killed, 2130 meters (7000 feet) of the railroad destroyed, and an entire section of the town buried. People couldn't help but wonder… could the rest of the mountain fall?

The first government inspectors arrived in June, two months after the slide, and confirmed the fears. A second slide could destroy the rest of the town at any moment, they warned. Still, the railroad was repaired, the road rebuilt, and the mine reopened.

In 1910, the government sent another team to decide whether continued mining was safe. The team's report read:

A large slide would cut off all railway communication and close the mines West of Frank. It might permanently close the pass. The town of Frank would be wiped
out with a fearful toll of life. These are some of the risks
that are being taken by tampering with the foundation
of this mountain.

The report also warned the local mining company that it would be held responsible if people died in a second slide. Still, the mine remained open.

More researchers arrived. In 1912, geologists pointed out new fissures that had opened near the top of the mountain, sending rocks and trees sliding at extreme angles. They warned that the peak was formed of layers of shale, coal, and limestone—layers that were just waiting for an excuse to slide. In 1918, the mine finally closed its doors forever.

A century later, scientists continue to watch the mountain, still debating the causes of the 1903 disaster. Many now believe that although the mountain was unstable and the mine's massive caverns would have weakened it further, some unusual event must have happened to trigger such a catastrophic slide. Perhaps a small earthquake shook the area or abrupt changes in temperature caused ice to expand and contract deep within the rock. Some believe that if a similar event triggered a new slide, it could be even larger than the first.

In 2005, a company called APEC drilled a shaft deep into the mountain and implanted $1 million of monitoring equipment. With satellites, the company can now use thousands of pinpoints on the mountainside to track tiny shifts in the rock. Hopefully, the scattering of residents who still live in the shadow of Turtle Mountain will have warning if the mountain decides to walk again.

Operation Gwamba

Surinam River, Surinam, 1964

JOHN WALSH WAS MOTORING DOWN the flooded river with his assistant, Willem "Wimpy" Aniset Pansa, when they spotted a tiny ball of orange fur high on the branches of an almost submerged tree. Grabbing some dangling vines, they yanked on the branches until the creature plopped into the water beside them. Quickly, Wimpy scooped it up with a net and rolled it onto the bottom of the dugout canoe.

As the tiny animal righted itself and shook off the water, John identified it as a pygmy anteater—the first one he'd seen since arriving in the jungles of Surinam. He couldn't resist picking it up. After all, he knew that anteaters had no teeth, and this one was only the size of his hand.

It wrapped its tail around one of his fingers and balanced on his palm, eyeing him. Then it raised its clutched paws to its nose.

How cute, thought John. It looks like it's praying.

Slash!

The anteater had not been praying after all; it had been preparing to attack. Attached to those paws were two razor-sharp claws, perfect for knifing into termite nests and scooping out the anteater's favorite food. And now these two claws had ripped parallel wounds into John's wrist.

As the anteater reared up to strike a second time, John quickly grabbed it by the tail and stuffed it into a small animal trap, then turned to wrap his bleeding wrist with a spare handkerchief.

Wimpy, meanwhile, was bent double with laughter. His boss, the snake-wrestling, panther-hunting man with the tranquilizer gun and the modern animal rescue equipment, had just been felled by a miniature anteater.

TWENTY-THREE-YEAR-OLD JOHN WALSH was an officer with the Massachusetts Society for the Prevention of Cruelty to Animals (SPCA) who specialized in investigating complaints. He had trained in police work, evidence collecting, veterinary medicine, and animal rescue techniques, but he had rarely left the United States. Then, on March 9, 1964, he was called into his boss's office, where he read a letter from the Surinam SPCA.

The letter explained that a Surinam aluminum company, in partnership with an American company, had dammed the Upper Surinam River to build a hydroelectric power plant. A massive swath of rainforest—about 14 times the area of John's home city of Boston—was about to be flooded.

"OUR SOCIETY IS SURE that animal-friends throughout the world will feel pity for the anteaters, for the deer, the tapirs, the sloths, the tree-porcupines, the howler- and the spider-monkeys, the smaller sakis and many more animals of the tropical rain forest, who are threatened by drowning or starvation… Time is short and the water rises."

JOHN HAD NEVER EVEN HEARD OF Surinam until his boss pointed it out on a map. It was a small country on the northern coast of South America, with Guyana to the west and Brazil to the south. And a moment later, John learned why his boss had called him. The International Society for the Protection of Animals (ISPA) wanted to send a representative to the area to rescue as many animals as possible from the flooded area and release them on the new shoreline. They had chosen John to go.

Less than a month later, he found himself in South America, standing on a newly built dam and surveying a sinking world. Because the new dam blocked much of the river, the valley behind it was slowly becoming an enormous lake. Over the next year and a half, as the dam neared completion and more water accumulated behind it, all sign of the vibrant rainforest would disappear. Already, the lower elevations had been flooded, leaving only the once lush treetops reaching from the water. Hilltops had become islands, and as the flooding continued these islands would become smaller and smaller. Some animals would be able to swim to other islands and eventually to the shoreline, but many creatures would not be able to swim such distances. They would be trapped on shrinking islands with dwindling food until they starved to death. Or until John saved them.

But what kind of animals would he be saving? How many creatures lived in that part of the jungle? John's boss merely shook his head. No one had ever researched the jungle populations of Surinam, so there were no details about the number of animals or the variety of species. All he could tell John was to save whatever creatures he could find, whether they were rare and exotic mammals or poisonous snakes.

Equipped with basic animal nets and traps from the SPCA, John set about hiring a crew of the Saramacca people who lived along the river. He had his workers buy or build two- and three-person dugout canoes, build a base camp in the midst of the jungle, and begin rescuing species of animals that John had never seen or even heard of before. He named his mission Operation Gwamba, using the local word for wild animal.

Slow Starts and Fast Attacks

The rescue operation began slowly. John and Wimpy—the first of the crew members—started by mapping parts of the giant lake where animals were most likely to be stranded. Then, on one of their mapping excursions, they found their first creature in distress. Stranded on the upper branches of a dead and sinking tree was a three-toed sloth, slowly starving to death. John gently detached it from its perch and paddled it to the shore. Once released, the animal escaped up the nearest tree at top sloth speed—it took more than 15 minutes.

Many of John's rescues were destined to be more dangerous. The river waters of Surinam were home to both piranhas and venomous snakes, the jungle floors hosted poisonous spiders and centipedes, and the treetops housed vampire bats that sometimes crept into tents at night to feed off blood. It was up to John and his team to paddle to a new island, sweep through the underbrush of the slowly disappearing rainforest, collect every animal possible, and transport them to safety.

One afternoon the dugout canoes were already loaded with captured deer, agoutis (rodents that look like large squirrels), and pacas (a smaller rodent cousin), when John heard one of his men yelling from the island where they had all been working. The man had spotted an ocelot, a medium-sized wildcat that hunts rodents, rabbits, and even deer. This one was leaping through the treetops, almost as comfortable there as it would have been on the ground.

Knowing the ocelot wouldn't survive on the shrinking island, about 10 men spread out in a loose semicircle and began to herd the cat toward the open water. Soon, it was perched in the tree-tops over the flood. Paddling after it in their dugouts, the crew chopped down every tree within jumping distance, effectively trapping the animal.

To get it down, John hoped to spear it with a tranquilizer dart. But the darts were always hard to use in the jungle, bouncing off rubbery leaves and rarely hitting their targets. To give John's shot a better chance, his crew began hewing branches off the ocelot's tree.

The cat attacked. Claws out, it launched itself at one of the men. Fortunately, that man's partner had a paddle in hand and was able to spin the boat. In the same moment, the targeted man leaped into the water on one side of the dugout while the ocelot fell sputtering on the other. Seconds later, it had scrambled back to its high perch.

It was time to try the tranquilizer gun, but the first shot missed, along with the second. Finally, the third shot managed to clear the twigs and branches and hit the cat in the thigh. It lowered itself to sleep, still on the branch.

The men hacked at the tree with their machetes until it lurched into the water, depositing the ocelot into the flood. Immediately, the animal sprang to life, clawing and churning its way through the water in a panicked attempt to escape the men. Braving the chance that piranhas would be attracted by the splashing, John leaped into the lake and managed to dodge the cat's claws long enough to grip the back of its neck and heave it into one of the boats. There, the men quickly slipped it into a sack and gave it another tranquilizer to prevent it from slicing through the canvas.

Once they reached shore and released the smaller animals, the crew laid a log to form a bridge between the dugout and the land. Then they untied the sack and retreated. A few minutes later, the ocelot streaked into the jungle, a blur of fur and muscle once again bound for the treetops.

WHILE THE OCELOT was one of the most rare and fascinating animals that John found in the jungle, it wasn't the largest creature captured. Along with giant turtles and armadillos, his men were faced with rescuing stranded tapirs using only their canoes.

Slightly larger than a Shetland pony and looking like a cross between a boar and an anteater, the tapir is actually related to the rhinoceros. Along the Surinam River, the animals fed on jungle fruit and leaves or on underwater plants. But there weren't many tapirs in the area, so when John's crew flushed the first one from the trees, it took him a moment to identify it.

He didn't have long to ponder. Squealing, the ungainly creature crashed through the underbrush, across the shore, and into the water, disappearing below the surface. Several boat-lengths away, its snorkel-like nose surfaced as it paddled as quickly as possible away from the rescue team.

With much yelling and bumping of boats, the crew paddled after it, dropping animal-catching loops around its neck and slinging ropes around its body. Almost immobilized, the tapir still managed to fight, whipping its snout over the side of a canoe and tearing out a chunk with its teeth, then puncturing another canoe with a well-aimed kick. It took four men struggling in the water, trying to maintain their grip as they were jerked back and forth by the animal's powerful kicks, just to tie the tapir's hind legs together.

When the animal was finally quiet, the crew faced another problem. It was too big to heave into a canoe. How would they transport it to shore? At first, they tried roping the animal between four boats, but the dead trees and logs that choked the flooded water made it impossible to paddle the four boats evenly side by side.

Wimpy finally found the solution when he happened to

glance at the pile of inflatable lifejackets inside his dugout. Back in the water, the men slid a chain of tied-together lifejackets around the tapir and inflated them. Soon, the creature was floating halfway out of the water like a giant tapir raft. By towing it behind one of the canoes, they managed to safely get it to shore.

Alone in the Jungle

Rescuing large animals was difficult enough as a team, but John occasionally found himself alone. As he was motoring from the camp to the dam at dusk one day, he spotted a deer swimming for its life in the open water. Knowing the shore was 32 kilometers (20 miles) away in that particular direction, he felt compelled to try to save it. He pulled his canoe alongside, close enough to reach down and touch the deer in the water. The animal was too tired to protest or try to escape.

Usually, the crew used donated nylon stockings to restrain deer—ropes were too harsh and would cut through the animals' skin. But John had no stockings with him. And he couldn't lift the deer onboard all by himself. So, stripping off his shirt, he pushed the deer's forelegs through the sleeves, buttoned it up down the back, and hooked his anchor chain through the shirt. Then, with the chain attached to the back of the dugout, he set off toward shore. With one hand, he held the motor and attempted to steer. With the other hand, he reached into the water to steady the frightened deer's head.

His system worked for about half the trip—until the dugout hit a submerged log. Suddenly the boat was jolted sideways and John was thrown into the lake. Before he could even get his bearings, the canoe had righted itself and was motoring away from him, the deer still attached to the side.

John was immediately concerned for the deer, then he

realized where he was: stranded. In the middle of the lake. His crew members thought he was away for the night and the men at the dam weren't expecting him. There would be no rescue boats coming, so there was nothing to do but swim.

For a few minutes, John managed to remain calm as he dog-paddled along, telling himself that although he probably couldn't make it the entire 16 kilometers (10 miles) to shore, he was sure to find a floating log or tiny island before that. Then it got darker. And he began thinking about the sunken villages and jungle growth underneath him, where piranhas gathered. Would it be long before he felt the first nip at his toes or his fingers? Would it be long after that when the entire school of fish arrived to strip the flesh off his body? Panicking, he began to thrash in the water, kicking as fast as he could. But just as quickly, he realized that his splashing might attract the fish. He slowed again. Maybe he would find the tops of some jungle trees still sticking out of the water, he thought. But they would be full of tarantulas and vampire bats. He kicked faster. Then he remembered the piranhas, and once again forced himself to slow down.

How much time had passed? John wondered. An hour? Two? Struggling to overcome his fear and wondering if an island would ever come into sight, John caught the faintest sound. It sounded like… a boat motor. Swimming as slowly and calmly as he could through the fading light, John at last saw safety. The dugout had snagged itself on an island of treetops and there it waited, the deer still attached to the side.

Feeling closer to death than he had ever been, John heaved himself up and into the canoe and lay panting on the bottom. Finally, with extreme caution, he backed out from the island, rebalanced the deer, and headed once more for shore.

Reptile Encounter

On another day, the dangers of the river sprang to life when one of the dogs John used to flush out game leaped into the water in pursuit of a paca. There was a sudden swirling of the water. Hardly able to believe their eyes, John and the crew watched as a giant anaconda—probably twice as long as a man—quickly slid its coils around the dog and pulled him under the surface.

Grabbing their paddles, the men rushed to the rescue. But by the time they got to the spot where the dog had disappeared, there was no sign of it. They searched the surrounding waters and the shore, but found nothing. The next day, one of the men boated by the island and spotted the anaconda lying in a thicket, a conspicuous bulge in its belly.

The Final Tally

Despite anacondas and piranhas, through monsoon rains and tropical fevers, John and his crew continued to work. By the time most islands were completely flooded and they had rescued all the animals they could find, John had been living in the jungle for a year and a half. He and his crew had saved a total of 9737 animals, not including small creatures such as toads and lizards. Included in the total were 2104 sloths, 671 deer, 528 monkeys, 518 porcupines, 261 anteaters, 167 snakes (including poisonous ones), and even one lost or abandoned housecat. Operation Gwamba was hailed in the media as the largest, most successful animal rescue in history.

John himself returned to Surinam's capital city shaking and quivering with the worst fever of his 18-month stay. He had been scratched by animals, infested with parasites, and bitten by vampire bats. At the local clinic, he was diagnosed with rabies, a disease that can easily prove fatal if not treated in 24 hours.

John had already been sick for more than five days.

Unable to get proper treatment in Surinam, he flew back to Boston where he was immediately hospitalized. And after several more days of fever and semi-consciousness, he was shaken awake by a doctor. He didn't have rabies after all—they had pinpointed his symptoms as those of bat salivary gland virus, a rare but not a life-threatening illness. He was going to live.

In fact, John would live to travel around the world for decades to come, saving thousands of other animals from danger. The group that sent John to the jungle is now called the World Society for the Protection of Animals and it campaigns internationally against such activities as factory farming, Asian bear farming, whale hunting, and bullfighting. John still works for the organization. One of his most recent assignments was to rescue abused animals in Afghanistan in 2002, including zoo animals who had been trapped in their cages on the front lines of a war. His work continues to reflect the advice his boss gave him before John embarked on Operation Gwamba in 1964—any animal, whether rare or common, passive or dangerous, has the right to live unthreatened by human activity.

Adrift on the Ice

The Arctic Circle near Norway, 1928

AT 12:24 A.M. ON MAY 25, after enduring 19 hours of wind and fog, the crew of the *Italia* stared below them in awe. They had done it. In the half-dark of the arctic night, they were bobbing in the air directly above the north pole. Leaning from the cabin into the cutting wind, Commander Umberto Nobile dropped a cross wrapped in an Italian flag onto the ice below.

"Viva Nobile!" A crew member let loose a boisterous cheer and soon shouts and laughter echoed through the vessel.

The *Italia* was an airship, or blimp, and one of the most advanced models in the world in 1928. It was essentially a giant, football-shaped bag filled with balloons of gas to keep it aloft. Inside its canvas skin, a rigid steel frame at the bow and stern helped the vessel hold its shape. In the bottom of the "football," just below the gas bags, a V-shaped steel frame allowed room for storage, sleeping quarters, and equipment. Attached below that was the cabin, 6 meters (20 feet) long and 2.4 meters (8 feet) wide, with the navigational equipment. Behind the cabin hung three powerful engines to drive the vessel through the air.

Umberto had been designing and building such vessels since he and three other engineers opened their own company in Italy ten years before. He had flown his airships in every possible weather condition, from hail to lightning storms. He had even written a textbook about aerodynamics. And two years before, he had joined forces with a famous Norwegian explorer named Roald Amundsen to attempt history's first flight to the north pole.

Although an airplane beat Umberto and Roald to the pole by three days on that trip, Umberto remained convinced that airships were the transportation wave of the future. After all, they could carry more cargo and passengers than planes could, they could fly farther, and they didn't need large airports for landing.

To help prove the usefulness of his airships and to satisfy his own thirst for adventure, Umberto had planned this second trip to the pole. This time, he took a crew of 16 men, including scientists who could land on the ice for several hours and take readings and measurements. Unfortunately, when the *Italia* finally reached the pole, the wind was too strong to lower the basket and allow the scientists onto the ice. After two hours of circling the area, the *Italia* turned and headed back toward their base at Spitsbergen, Norway.

THROUGHOUT THE RETURN TRIP, the weather grew steadily worse. Strong gusts of wind made the airship quiver and buck. Ice pellets began forming on the propellers and whipping off to hit the canvas, ripping small holes that the crew scrambled to patch. As the storm swelled, the wind pushed the vessel first one way, then the other. The engineers strained to stay on a straight course, but managed only to zig-zag back and forth through the air. At one point, the steering fins froze into place while the *Italia* was pointed nose down, sending the airship motoring toward the ice. Umberto frantically called an emergency stop to the engines, leaving the vessel to be buffeted by the wind while the men chipped the ice away.

To make matters worse, the navigation experts on board

could no longer pinpoint the *Italia's* exact location. In the days before radar or radio beacons, an airship's position was determined by measuring its distance from known landmarks. But in the Arctic Circle, the endless expanses of ice looked exactly the same—there *were* no landmarks. The pilots on board could rely on the stars instead, but frequent clouds and fog made the method unreliable. To compensate, the crew of the *Italia* used compasses, wind direction, ground speed, and their last known location to constantly calculate their position. To measure their altitude, they dropped small "bombs" of red dye onto the ice below, measuring the amount of time between the drop and the splash. But because of the constant bucking of the wind and the looming banks of fog, all of these methods were proving useless.

Convinced that the storm would eventually subside and determined to reach port, Umberto tried every available option. He tried to lift the airship above the fog, he tried to maintain a steady altitude below the fog, and he tried different engine speeds to stop the constant bucking. But after eight hours of flight, the crew was exhausted and the wind showed no signs of abating.

At 10:05 a.m., the stern of the airship suddenly rose in the air, pointing the bow directly toward the ice. Umberto ordered the engines at full power ahead, and the rudders turned to point the airship upward. There was no change. He tried to turn the airship aside, in case it was simply caught in a downdraft of air. Again, there was no change. Was gas escaping from a rip at the rear of the vessel or from a faulty valve? No one would ever find out. Before the mechanics could check, the ice was already rising to meet the airship. Fast.

There was nothing to do but prepare for a crash. To lower the risk of fire, the crew cut power to the engines. Umberto rushed to help a crew member hold the wheel steady. Through the glass cabin windows, he could see the ice rushing toward him a moment before the impact. Then a piece of the frame crashed down on his head, his body was thrown forward through the cables and canvas, and he heard the snap of a bone in his leg as he fell.

"S.O.S. Italia. Save Our Souls!"

As the ship struck with a screech of bending steel and scraping ice, ten of the crew members, including Umberto, tumbled out of the cabin. Only six remained on board. Of those, one was uninjured and alert enough to begin throwing emergency supplies onto the ice—a tent, sleeping bags, a gun, dye, smoke signals, a stove, fuel, and rations. But the wind was still howling and the airship, without all the equipment, was growing steadily lighter. With horror, the men on the ground watched as a sudden gust picked up the wreckage and spun it away from the ice, with the crew members still on board. Before anyone had time to react, the damaged airship was high in the air once more, and floating from sight.

The men were now stranded on the unstable pack ice that constantly circled the north pole, carried by the Arctic currents. One crew member lay dead, several—including Umberto—had broken bones, and no one knew their coordinates. Without coordinates, search planes looking for stranded men on the vast Arctic ice would be like spectators looking for toothpicks on an Olympic hockey rink—from the top bleachers. In fact, even the *Italia* crew didn't know exactly where they were, except that they were somewhere northeast of Spitsbergen.

Still, the crew members had been chosen for the voyage because of their proven intelligence and endurance. Those who were unhurt wrapped Umberto and another badly injured man in a sleeping bag, then began gathering the supplies from the ice.

They collected warm clothes, navigation equipment, charts, a tent, a gun, an ax, and enough food to sustain the nine of them for 45 days. One of the radio operators had been thrown from the cabin while clutching a small, battery-powered radio to his chest. It still seemed to work.

Within a day, the men had set up the tent and dyed it red with altitude bombs to help make it easier for searchers to spot. They had also taken navigational readings and tried to locate their position on the charts. With their approximate coordinates, they began trying the radio: "S.O.S. *Italia*! Save our Souls!"

Missing in Action

When the *Italia* failed to return to port the next day as expected, word spread quickly along the northern coast of Europe. The disappearance could only mean one thing: the airship had crashed. Explorers, sailors, pilots, and government officials in Norway, Sweden, the Netherlands, and Finland began to talk about rescue plans, while whaling and fishing boats were put on alert for any sign of the wreckage.

There were two problems. First, it was late spring, so the northern ice was breaking into a dangerous jigsaw puzzle of icebergs and open water. With no known location for the survivors amidst the shifting ice, the searchers had no idea where to start. Second, the Italian government had not sanctioned Umberto's voyage. (In fact, after Umberto had refused to hand his airship manufacturing plant over to the government several years before, officials seemed determined to ignore the engineer's existence.) An Italian ship in Spitsbergen was supposed to act as a base for the *Italia*, but the ship's captain was convinced that the airship could never have survived the Arctic storms. He didn't even bother to monitor the emergency radio frequencies.

Without the Italian government coordinating rescue attempts, officials from other countries seemed unsure of how to help. After all, it was likely the crew members of the *Italia* were dead, lost forever in the Arctic. For days, rescuers did nothing except talk, until it seemed as if Europe would bypass a rescue operation and move directly into mourning the dead.

An Endless March

As more than a week went by with no signs that the radio was working or that rescue efforts were underway, the mood among the survivors on the ice turned sour. Some battled with depression, convinced that they would die. Others were determined to save themselves without waiting for rescue.

Knowing the dangers of drifting ice, sudden storms, and polar bears, Umberto was reluctant to send men to try to walk to the mainland. Finally, however, he was convinced that to order strong and healthy men to stay quietly on the ice and wait would only cause conflict among his crew. Two Italian navy engineers and a Swedish meteorologist, Finn Malmgren, set off with their share of the rations and an ax for protection. They aimed for the closest solid land, Foyn Island. From there, they could plan a second march to an inhabited island.

Almost immediately, the trek became grueling. Finn had injured his shoulder and his kidney in the crash, and the constant walking made the pain flare. Then, after several days on the open ice, a storm left them huddled for 48 hours in a little shelter they managed to chop. When the wind finally abated, they found that they had drifted even farther from Foyn Island. All their previous walking had been useless.

Still, they set out again. The walked all day, every day, sometimes marching for 15 hours straight. As time passed, Malmgren began falling behind. The constant pain clouded his mind, and he became more and more convinced that he had failed the *Italia* crew and his entire country of Sweden by not taking better weather readings and predicting the strength of the storm that had caused the crash. With frostbitten feet and hands, he collapsed again and again, only to be hauled up by his two companions. Finally, on the fourteenth day of the march, he could only lie on the ice semi-conscious, begging to be left behind. Knowing that this was their only option if any of them were going to survive, the Italians fashioned a rough trench to protect him from the wind, left him pemmican and a fresh-water icicle, and marched on.

The two remaining men were in rough shape as well. The constant glare of the Arctic sun on the ice began to cause snow-blindness. After three weeks of marching, one man went completely blind for several days and had to be led by the hand across the ice. Often, the blind man splashed through puddles, and soaking his feet led quickly to frostbite. Meanwhile, Foyn Island continued to fade farther away as the ice drifted.

Then one of the men slipped and wrenched his leg. Admitting defeat, they made a rough camp and hoped for rescue. On June 30, they divided their last rations. Soon, they could only lie quietly out of the wind, aching with cold and hunger.

Attempted Rescues

Unbeknownst to the two starving men, rescue attempts had begun about three weeks earlier. On June 6, a young Soviet farmer and amateur radio operator received a transmission that dramatically changed the situation on the mainland. He heard the emergency radio signal of the survivors. Immediately, he contacted the Soviet government, which in turn contacted the Italians. Finally, on June 8, almost two weeks after the crash, the Italian base ship reported that it had received Umberto's S.O.S. transmission and knew his coordinates. Shortly after, the survivors on the ice received their first radio message—rescuers were on the way.

On June 10, the Russian icebreaker *Krassin* left port in Leningrad and headed for Norway. Several ships and planes closer to the crash site began sweeps of the area. But still the Italian's base ship sat inactive in port, the captain unwilling to risk his crew to help with the rescue efforts.

One man in particular was infuriated by this. Captain Gennaro Sora was an Italian soldier and an expert alpine skier whose ski team had been brought along by Umberto to help transport supplies and assist if a rescue was needed. Now, when a rescue apparently *was* needed, Gennaro was told by the base ship that the conditions were too dangerous. When he planned to lead a rescue mission without authorization, he was threatened with a court-martial.

He went anyway.

Leaving his men behind to save them from the army's displeasure, he joined forces with a Danish engineer and a Dutch explorer. On June 18, the three men set out from Norway by dogsled. Within a few days, the engineer was suffering from snow-blindness and stomach cramps. Leaving him to make his way back to Norway with a two-week supply of rations, Gennaro and his Dutch partner, Sjef van Dongen, continued. They were caught for two days in a storm and two injured dogs had to be shot, but still they persevered. Even after a search plane dropped a warning about the fragile condition of the ice, the men pressed on.

To reach the survivors in the red tent, Gennaro and Sjef needed to take their dogsled across the patchy ice floes, or moving ice islands, between land and the more permanently frozen pack ice around the pole. But when they got to the edge of the land, they could find no solid route to the pack ice. In the end, they chose what looked like the most stable "island" of floating ice and took the dogs and the sled onto it, hoping it would bump against the more solid pack ice on the other side, allowing them to pick their way across.

Almost as soon as they had crossed to the floe, it split beneath them with a deafening crack, leaving Gennaro, the sled, and two dogs on one side of a widening chasm of water, and Sjef and the other dogs on the far side. Sjef quickly leaped across the gap as the island pulled itself apart, but the dogs, still roped together, were dragged into the water. The sled slipped in after them, held half afloat by the air in the sleeping bags and storage bags.

Every second, the situation grew more chaotic. The panicked dogs tangled themselves in their harnesses, while Gennaro and Sjef slipped and struggled on the wet ice. In the midst of the confusion, Sjef managed to grab one of the ropes, swim across the open water to solid land, and start to heave the sled toward him. Gennaro flopped onto his stomach to help untangle the ropes, then eventually jumped into the water to help push the sled along. They managed to get it back to land, with two of the dogs still attached. The other five had been swept away by the current, along with most of the men's supplies.

Completely soaked, Gennaro and Sjef were left with one week of food and one wet sleeping bag between them. They decided to set out for Foyn Island, where the search planes would be closest. Ironically, the two rescuers were already relatively close to Foyn Island, while the men who had set off from the *Italia* crash site had by now drifted several days to the east.

Leaving the dogsled behind and trying to stay in constant motion to keep their wet clothes from freezing, the two were able to leap across a different set of ice floes and onto the ice pack.

On July 4, they reached Foyn Island, swimming the last distance to shore and soaking themselves again. By the time they arrived, Sjef was vomiting and delirious with a high fever and Gennaro was hypothermic and weak.

For eight days, they huddled together on the island, until they had only half a chocolate bar left between them.

Searchers in the Air

Although Gennaro wasn't the only searcher to consider dogsleds, most experts thought that a small plane would be most likely to successfully find and retrieve the *Italia* survivors. With this plan in mind, explorer Roald Amundsen had set out in a French plane on June 16. Because of a lack of funding, the plane was not ideal for polar conditions. To make matters worse, the six men on board overloaded the small craft, and their radio transmitter was too weak for the vast Arctic distances. Roald and his crew were never seen again.

Fortunately, other teams were better equipped. In the third week of June, two Norwegian, two Italian, a Swedish, and a Finnish plane all began sweeps of the area. With no country taking control of the search, the pilots organized their routes separately, without dividing the area in any way. Still, they managed to criss-cross a patch of the immense Arctic. Below them, in every direction, bumpy, curled chips of glaciers and flat expanses of sea ice made a crazy puzzle out of the ocean. They flew in slow circles, constantly squinting, hoping for any small flash of color. Because of the *Italia's* continued radio transmissions, they knew they were looking for a red tent.

On the afternoon of June 17, Umberto and the five other men remaining at the tent heard the steady buzz of two approaching planes. Desperately trying to start a signal fire and waving their most brightly colored shirts in the air, they shouted frantically at the pilots, only to collapse in frustration when the aircrafts circled in the other direction.

Still, the survivors were able to radio Norway and tell officials that two planes had passed near the camp. Because the pilots knew where they had turned around, they were able to pinpoint the red tent's location. Three days later, a break in the weather allowed an Italian plane to circle low overhead. Although the aircraft was too heavy to land on the unstable ice, it was able to drop food and supplies. The next day more food arrived, along with medicine, shoes, batteries for the dying radio, and even letters from home.

Though buoyed by the new supplies, the survivors were becoming more desperate. The surface beneath them was weakening in the summer weather, and every day new puddles formed. At any moment, their patch of ice could crack open, plunging the entire camp into the water.

The same fear plagued rescue pilots. If they touched down on the ice pack, would it crack beneath them and send the plane into the sea?

Hoping that someone would be brave enough to at least try, the survivors searched for the flattest, most stable-looking strip of ice in their vicinity, marking it with dyed red fabric. Perhaps, in a small plane, one of the pilots would be skilled enough to land. A Swedish war veteran named Einar Lundborg took up the challenge.

Setting out from Norway at 10 p.m. on June 23 and taking advantage of the Arctic summer's constant light, he landed an hour later on the bumpy makeshift runway. His aircraft was light enough to risk the weak ice, but only large enough to carry one survivor. Despite Umberto's protests, Einar insisted that the airship commander leave the camp first—not only was he the most badly injured, he would also be the most helpful in looking for the three men who had tried to march to safety.

The five others watched the plane depart, hoping for its quick return. Six hours later, they again heard the buzz of the engine. But instead of landing at one end of the runway, this time the plane touched down in the center. The pilot hadn't slowed down enough when he approached, and the aircraft smashed into a crack in the ice and flipped, landing upside down with a damaged propeller. The pilot (who survivors later claimed was drunk at the time) was now stranded on the ice as well.

Although several more pilots attempted the flight in the following days, bad weather kept forcing them back to Norway. Finally, a week after the plane crash and more than a month after the *Italia* went down, a small Swedish plane came and retrieved the stranded pilot. But the ice conditions were now even worse and the searchers were themselves exhausted. Swedish officials decided that while they could keep dropping supplies, it was no longer safe to attempt landings on the ice.

The Icebreaker

That left the survivors with one last hope. On June 24, two weeks after the Russian icebreaker *Krassin* had left Leningrad, it had pulled away from port in Bergen, Norway. The ship had been out of service for two years and was encrusted with layers of rust and coal dust, but it was still the most powerful icebreaker in Europe. Heavy-duty engines and a steel hull could push icebergs aside and power through thick pack ice.

As it crossed the floes, the ship would accelerate at full power, churning over the ice until the bow stuck into the air. Then the ice would shatter beneath it, plunging the vessel back into the water. For the sailors on board, this method meant seasickness and deafening noise, but the ship slowly made progress.

On June 30, as the *Krassin* finally smashed its way into the right area of the Arctic, search planes provided the captain with the latest coordinates of the red tent. Then one search plane found two other survivors, trapped on an ice floe surrounded by open water. The pilot relayed exact coordinates, but had to make an emergency landing a short distance away because of fog. The plane's propellers were damaged, and the plane crew was now trapped on the ice as well.

It took three days for the *Krassin* to crush its way along an altered course to the men on the ice floe. As soon as a lookout spotted a man staggering on the ice, the ship creaked to a stop. The captain didn't dare risk powering too close, in case the ship split the ice underneath the survivors. When a rescue party climbed down a ladder from the deck and hurried toward the survivors, one fell into their arms. The other was too weak to stand, or even recognize that rescuers had arrived. These were the men who had set off from the *Italia*'s crash site weeks before. It had been thirteen days since their last meal. No trace of the Swedish meteorologist was ever found.

Within an hour, the *Krassin* was back underway. But now the captain faced a difficult choice. Lookouts had spotted two men signaling for help from Foyn Island—almost certainly Gennaro and his dogsled crew. The *Krassin* was already low on coal. Should the ship aim for Gennaro, for the stranded Russian search plane crew, or for the red tent? Deciding that Gennaro, at least, was safe on land and wouldn't be drifting, and that the search plane crew was well supplied and safe as well, the captain aimed for the coordinates of the red tent.

By that afternoon, the five survivors still at the original *Italia* crash site saw what must have seemed like a hallucination—a massive steel hull powering through the ice toward them. It was 49 days after the airship crash.

Once the survivors were on board, the *Krassin* stopped to collect the Russian search plane crew, then motored its way back to Norway.

The captain received word that a search plane had spotted Gennaro and Sjef and had managed to land near Foyn Island and retrieve them. Gennaro, though threatened again with a court-martial when he returned to base, was never actually punished for his actions.

The Aftermath

Three whaling ships continued to scan the Arctic waters for weeks, looking for Roald Amundsen's plane and for the *Italia* wreckage. Despite their efforts, no sign was ever found of the *Italia* or the six men swept away with the airship. As for Roald and his crew, only one clue surfaced. On an island in northern Norway, a single seaplane float was found washed up on the rocks, looking as if it had been torn from a plane by the force of a crash.

During these final days of the search, Umberto and his seven surviving crew members were ushered straight from the *Krassin* onto an Italian train. In the opinion of the Italian government, the *Italia* voyage had been a complete disgrace—both a scientific failure and a botched rescue. Officials banned any welcome parties for the survivors.

On board the train, shut off from friends, family, and the media, the survivors worried about what to expect. But just as people like Roald and Gennaro had formed independent rescue teams when the Italian government failed to act, the citizens of Italy chose their own courses of action.

As the train pulled up to the first Italian station platform, a crowd shouted and cheered a greeting. At the next platform, another welcoming crowd waited. Then another, and another. By the time the train reached Rome, news of the survivors' arrival had spread: there were 200,000 people gathered at the station to welcome them home.

Deadline for Death

Mogadishu, Somalia, October 1977

THE PASSENGERS WHO BOARDED Lufthansa Flight 181 on October 13, 1977, were tanned and smiling. Majorca, Spain, was a Mediterranean vacation hotspot, and the airport was almost as relaxed as the rest of the island. Security staff checked some bags, but not all, and latecomers were cheerfully waved through the line.

Christine Santiago, an Austrian–American woman, made her way down the aisle, stowed her carry-on bag, and helped settle her five-year-old son, Leo, into his seat. Three young German girls sat nearby, chatting and laughing. An elderly couple sat a few rows behind. Six tall, gorgeous women filed by. They were German beauty pageant winners, another passenger whispered, on their way back from enjoying a prize-package holiday.

Just as the plane doors were about to shut, four young people rushed aboard, laughing and apologizing for their lateness. They were good-natured and friendly, the three men patting a few children on the heads as they rushed down the aisle, the woman smiling at the passengers around her. One of the newcomers even held a crying baby while its mother organized her luggage.

Without further delay, the airplane doors closed, the flight attendants began their safety instructions, and the jet took off for Frankfurt, Germany.

A New Captain

Less than an hour later, as the flight attendants finished serving lunch, those same four latecomers raced down the aisle of the plane, waving pistols and grenades and shouting in Arabic. The passengers, who just a few minutes before had been enjoying their memories of relaxing vacations, were now the hostages of Palestinian terrorists.

Many of the people on the plane had only a vague understanding of the political situation in the Middle East. A few of them knew that after World War II, the United Nations had divided part of the Middle East into two separate states, one for Jews (Israel) and one for Arabs (Palestine). And they might have remembered that the Arab nations of the region refused to accept the plan, and attacked Israel. After the Arab defeat, the section of the territory that had been Palestine was divided between Israel, Egypt, Syria, and Jordan, and the independent state of Palestine was lost.

What *all* the passengers knew was that terrorism was becoming more and more common. A few people had turned to violent methods to try to get the state of Palestine back, attacking innocent people to gain the attention of the media and international governments.

On board Flight 181, Christine found herself in the middle of one such attack. She clutched her son as one of the terrorists, bushy-haired and stocky, shouted at the passengers in rough English. His name, he announced, was Captain Mahmoud. He was the new captain of the plane, he was taking over the flight, and he was going to kill anyone who moved. To Christine, it seemed as if every second word he said was "execute."

Quickly, she and the passengers around her did as they were told. They threw the plastic knives and forks they had been using to eat their lunches into the center aisle. A hijacker quickly col lected them. Next, the passengers handed over their passports and identification papers. The terrorists examined these closely, assessing which passengers might be the most dangerous, and which were rich, or famous, or important in political circles. Every passenger with some sort of fame or status would give the hijackers more power during ransom negotiations.

Christine struggled to stay calm for the sake of her son. But soon, her attention was drawn by a commotion. One of the terrorists was hauling the three girls, the ones who had been laughing and chatting earlier, into the aisle. Captain Mahmoud was screaming at them. What was he saying?

Jewish.

It seemed that Captain Mahmoud believed the three girls were Jewish.

"You will be executed at 8 tomorrow," he shouted. Then, in one of the abrupt mood changes that would keep the passengers on edge for the entire ordeal, Mahmoud suddenly calmed down, smiled to the surrounding passengers, and gently waved the three girls back to their seats. He wouldn't be killing them, he explained, because he was a freedom fighter. He wasn't a terrorist.

CAPTAIN SCHUMANN, a 37-year-old father of two and the real captain of Flight 181, obeyed Mahmoud's order to turn the plane toward Rome. He had already listened to Mahmoud's ranting, and he had watched as the hijacker slapped the co-pilot, ripping off the man's watch and crushing it because it showed a star that may have been the Star of David, a Jewish symbol.

Captain Schumann took a deep breath and remembered a conversation he'd had with his wife just weeks before. If you ever hear that my plane has been hijacked, he'd said, try to stay calm. I'm not the type for dangerous heroics.

He flinched as the terrorists waved their guns past his head to point them at the jet's radio operator. Sweating under the multiple barrels, the operator radioed Rome. Without actually using the word "hijacked," he told the control tower that his flight was under new leadership. It was being diverted and would need to land.

A Government in Crisis

West German Chancellor Helmut Schmidt was in his office on the afternoon of October 13, preparing to meet with his top officials about the recent kidnapping of an important German businessman. The businessman had already been missing for more than a month and the kidnappers were demanding the release of 11 political prisoners from German jails.

What could he do? Release murderers in exchange for the businessman's life? Allow the man's family to pay millions of dollars in ransom money? Refuse to negotiate with the terrorists? Schmidt and his officials couldn't seem to make a decision, and the German newspapers were haranguing them for their failures.

Now, Schmidt received a call to tell him that another international crisis loomed—82 terrified passengers and five crew members were on board a German plane that had been hijacked by terrorists.

Once the plane landed in Rome, Schmidt learned that the hijackers were demanding the release of 11 political prisoners—the same ones who were being demanded by the kidnappers. Could the two groups be connected?

Schmidt had no way of knowing, but he was sure of one thing—this time, there would be no long weeks of meandering negotiations. He was going to take action quickly. The hijackers were demanding he release the prisoners by noon on October 16, or they would kill all the hostages and blow up the plane. Schmidt had three days.

"This time we stand firm," he said to one of his aides. "Nothing will shake us."

SCHMIDT AND ONE OF HIS TOP MINISTERS—Werner Maihofer—sprang into action. As the plane touched down in Rome, they pleaded with the Italian government to prevent another take-off. Shoot out the plane's tires, they suggested. Anything to keep the plane and the hostages in one place, on the ground.

Maihofer also called on the West German border police, the force responsible for overseeing airline security issues. Ever since Palestinian terrorists had murdered eight Israeli athletes at the 1972 Olympics in Munich, a special section of the border police had been training in counter-terrorism.

When Maihofer reached Ulrich Wegener, the slim 48-year-old in charge of the commando unit, he had only one thing to say: "You have an important job to do."

For Wegener, it was the call he had waited five years to receive. Since his unit was established, they had trained in martial arts, practiced rappelling from helicopters, and learned to use the world's most advanced anti-terrorist weapons. They had formed teams of weapons, explosives, and communications specialists. Together, they had practiced bursting into locked rooms, overtaking mock terrorists, and rescuing mock hostages.

Once they were called into action, Wegener and his commando team were airborne and bound for Rome within hours. But before they landed, Italian officials gave in to the hijackers' demands for fuel and allowed the jet to take off.

The hijacked jet landed again that night in Cyprus with the

commando plane following close behind, but the island authorities there didn't want the responsibility for making decisions that would risk the lives of the hostages. They denied the German commandos permission to attempt a rescue operation, and forced them to land at a base an hour away from the main airport.

At 10:50 p.m. on October 13, the hijackers again took off with a full tank of fuel. After a stop in Bahrain, another small Middle Eastern country, they landed in the city of Dubai in the United Arab Emirates.

Back in Germany, Chancellor Schmidt tried a new tactic. He selected a top minister with strong Arab connections and sent him to join the commandos in Dubai and negotiate with the terrorists. Secretly, he gave his negotiator a second mission: work with two anti-terrorism specialists to draw as much information as possible from the hijackers, in the hope that the information would help Wegener's team of commandos plan a rescue.

Again, the rescue mission was thwarted at every turn. First, a high-ranking Dubai official demanded that his forces take part in any mission—but his forces weren't trained in this kind of anti-terrorism operation. Then the hijackers panicked and shot at airport engineers who approached the plane with a portable generator. Clearly, both the hijackers and the hostages were highly nervous. A badly timed rescue operation could prove disastrous.

Instead, negotiators asked the terrorists to release the women and children on board, and allow anyone ill to be taken to a local hospital. The terrorists refused and threatened to blow up the plane unless their demands for more fuel were met.

Fear and Claustrophobia

On board the plane, passenger Erno Kiralli tried gingerly to stretch his legs, extending one after the other as far as he could under the row in front of him. After long hours in his seat, his muscles seemed permanently cramped. The plane was like an oven, baking in the desert sun. To make matters worse, the toilets had overflowed, filling the air with the stench of sewage. All around him, it seemed that hungry, thirsty children were crying. Someone in the row across the aisle vomited, and Erno tried not to do the same.

Over the last few hours, Captain Mahmoud had grown more and more unpredictable. He paced the aisle, ranting about the industrialized world and explaining his opinions about the problems of Palestine. Then he stopped to order the Dubai control tower to send champagne and cake so he could celebrate the 28th birthday of one of the flight attendants. And after that, he was off on another rant.

Erno knew that the safest thing to do was stay as quiet as possible, avoiding the notice of the unpredictable hijackers. But he happened to glance up just as Captain Mahmoud paced by. Stopping abruptly, the hijacker stepped toward him and raised his pistol.

"I don't like your face," growled Captain Mahmoud.

Erno stared at the black metal barrel of the pistol, so scared that he couldn't move or speak. Then, a moment later, it was over. The hijacker resumed his pacing, and Erno tried to start breathing again.

In the cockpit, Captain Schumann was growing more desperate.

As the sun set on October 16, and the deadline for releasing

Germany's political prisoners passed, Captain Mahmoud grabbed the radio controls and screamed at the Dubai control tower, "I'm going to kill them all."

Schumann closed his eyes momentarily. They had been trapped in the plane for days, and there was no sign that the German government was working to free them. Without confronting the hijackers, Schumann had done everything possible to help potential rescuers. Thinking back to his anti-terrorism training, he had tried to leave signs and signals about the action inside. For example, just before the terrorists dumped trash onto the runway, he had dropped four unsmoked cigarettes into one of the garbage bags. If the rescuers outside were paying attention, clues like this one would tell them how many hijackers were on board.

But there seemed to be no response, and Schumann had no choice but to obey Captain Mahmoud's order to take off yet again. He turned the jet toward Aden, Southern Yemen. The local government there refused the jet permission to land and blockaded the runway with cement barriers. But Captain Schumann was low on fuel and desperately wanted to be on the ground, where rescuers had a chance of reaching the plane. Using all his skills, he made an emergency landing in the sandy strip alongside the runway.

Captain Mahmoud gave Schumann permission to leave the plane and check the landing gear for damage. But when Schumann returned, the hijacker was frantic. He accused Schumann of trying to escape, of trying to ruin the mission. He forced the pilot to his knees in front of the passengers.

"Are you guilty? Are you guilty?" he screamed.

Ignoring Schumann's pleas, Captain Mahmoud killed him with a single bullet to the head.

At 1 a.m. on October 17, with the pilot's corpse still lying on the floor, the copilot followed Captain Mahmoud's orders to take off from Aden and land in Mogadishu, the capital city of Somalia, a poor Arab country in northern Africa.

Shortly after they landed, the terrorists opened one of the emergency exits and shoved Schumann's body down the plastic chute and onto the tarmac. If the German negotiators weren't taking the terrorists' demands seriously, maybe a body would help.

Pleading for Action

With the pilot's death, the world suddenly began to pay major attention to the hijacked plane. Newspapers in every country covered the story, and world leaders began to demand action. The German negotiator begged the Somali president to endorse a rescue mission; diplomats from Britain, France, and the United States added their encouragement. Meanwhile, working on a different tack, Pope Paul VI publicly offered to board the jet and allow himself to be held hostage if the hijackers released the passengers and crew.

Finally, the Somali president—a man some believed was a warlord hoping to gain goodwill and weapons shipments by cooperating with the Western countries—gave his permission. The commandos could at last attack the plane directly and try to save the hostages and seize the terrorists. To the outside world, it seemed like an impossible task. But to the commandos, it was the chance to put all their training into action.

By mid-morning on October 17, the German negotiator had taken up residence in the Mogadishu control tower and tried to resume talks with the hijackers. By now, however, the hijackers had lost faith. They no longer believed the Germans were going to meet their demands, and they began to prepare to turn their mission into a suicide bombing. Inside the plane, they planted plastic explosives. They ordered the female passengers to remove their stockings, then used the nylon to tie the hands of some of the men. Captain Mahmoud ran up and down the aisle sprinkling alcohol over the seats and the passengers, threatening to blow them all up in one massive explosion.

Suddenly, one final call came from the negotiator in the control room. Germany was releasing the 11 political prisoners. They would be flown to Mogadishu to meet the hijackers.

Ecstatic, Captain Mahmoud agreed to delay the burning of the jet by seven hours, the time it would take to fly in the prisoners. He turned to some of the passengers (the same ones he had just sprinkled with alcohol) and asked them not to be personally offended—his actions were all part of the necessary struggle against imperialist countries and Jewish people, he said. And as night fell, the hijackers on board finally began to relax. One even released the grenades he had been carrying, tossing them onto an empty seat.

IN THE DARKNESS, a single plane landed at the far side of the closed Mogadishu airport, its lights off and its shutters closed. It was the plane carrying the German commandos. Unnoticed by the hijackers, it taxied to the far end of the airport, flashed its lights once in a signal to the control tower, then waited.

A Burst of Light

Midnight passed. Moving in the dark, invisible even from the control tower, German commandos in camouflage gear slipped down the runway and crawled beneath the hijacked jet. Two groups silently propped plastic ladders against the rear doors, attaching explosives. Sharpshooters dropped to their bellies on the tarmac. Teams of soldiers waited under the tail of the plane.

Inside the cockpit, the radio crackled to life. It was the German negotiator from the control tower, calling to say there had been a delay in the release of the prisoners. Captain Mahmoud was furious. Immediately, he ordered the other three hijackers forward for a conference.

It was just as the commandos had hoped...

Moments after the negotiator's call, the explosives on the plane doors detonated with a thunderous bang. From the tarmac, the sharpshooters used their infrared sights to blow stun grenades through the now open doors.

Flash!

The plane was lit from within like a Christmas tree. The stun grenades, designed to blow up without producing shrapnel, created such a chaos of noise and light that the hijackers—and passengers—were momentarily deaf and blind.

When Christine Santiago could see again, the first thing she focused on was a man with a greasepaint-smeared face bursting through the plane door.

"Get down! Get down!" he shouted in German.

On the other side of the aisle, another commando dove across a row of passengers, shouting the same thing.

One of the hijackers leaped down the aisle, and was quickly dropped by a burst of machine-gun fire from the commandos. Another hijacker met the same fate. Then Captain Mahmoud emerged from the cockpit. He was pulling the pin from a grenade, but he dropped it and it rolled toward the cockpit and detonated in the front of the plane without hurting anyone. As the commandos shot him down, Captain Mahmoud pulled the pin from a second grenade, throwing it with literally his last breath.

Miraculously, it rolled under the seats of the first-class section, detonating beneath the plush upholstery and cutting only the legs of a few nearby passengers.

In the command post outside, Wegener received word from his commando team.

"Springtime."

He smiled. That was the code word for success.

In seven minutes, the commandos had killed three of the hijackers, captured the fourth, and saved the lives of all passengers on board.

AT 2 A.M. ON OCTOBER 18, Chancellor Schmidt was still in his office. Since receiving the news about the hijacking five days before, he had slept for merely five hours. He had smoked dozens of cigarettes and drunk countless bottles of cola. But his fatigue was forgotten when he heard the voice of the German negotiator saying, "The job is done."

Although the hijackers spoke Arabic and many assumed that they were Palestinians, they carried no identification and no known terrorist group ever claimed responsibility for the hijacking. The one surviving hijacker, Suhaila Al-Sayeh, was carried from the plane on a stretcher, flashing a victory sign at onlookers and shouting "Palestine." She was held in a Somali prison for one year before the authorities there released her under mysterious circumstances. She was later recaptured in Norway and in 1996 was sentenced to a 12-year prison term in Germany.

FOR THE HOSTAGES, the ordeal was over. They struggled to move and walk after their long confinement, eager to get back to their families. The entire flight crew would receive the Cross of Merit, Germany's medal of bravery, when they returned home. Wegener received the same medal, along with a promotion to colonel.

But for Chancellor Schmidt, the problems of the past months were far from finished. Within an hour after news of the successful commando raid, 4 of the 11 political prisoners committed suicide in a German prison—their last protest for their cause. And the businessman who had been kidnapped weeks before was later found dead in France, with a note from the kidnappers saying that his death was hardly equal to the sadness they felt over the "murders" of the hijackers in Mogadishu.

In Germany, as in the rest of the world, the fight against terrorism was just beginning. Soon after this hijacking, the United States Congress issued warnings that airport security in Spain, Italy, France, and Greece was lax and dangerous. *Newsweek* magazine ran a story titled "The New War on Terrorism," and airline passengers around the world began to board their planes with less friendliness and more fear.

Lake Erie, November 24, 1854

CAPTAIN HACKETT LOOKED AT THE DARK LINE across the waters of Lake Erie and cursed the fickle November weather. When he and the crew of the *Conductor* had set out from Amherstberg, at the mouth of the Detroit River, the air over the Great Lakes had been cold but calm. Now the wind was picking up, dark clouds were rolling in, and night was falling. In his thick Scottish brogue, he shouted instructions to his crew. This wasn't the first storm he'd faced on the Great Lakes, and he was determined to see his shipment of grain safely to Port Dalhousie, Ontario.

But as the storm struck, just after nightfall, Captain Hackett began to wonder if he'd ever see the shore again. The air was frigid, even for November, and sleet sheeted from the skies. High winds whipped through the waves, picking up water and swirling it into an icy mist that made it impossible to see. Soon, heavy ice hung from the ship's deck and clung to the sails and rigging, pushing the *Conductor* lower in the water.

Although Lake Erie is the smallest of the five Great Lakes along the border between Canada and the United States, it is still the 13th largest natural lake in the world. It spans 25,700 square kilometers (9910 square miles), making it about six times larger than the state of Rhode Island. In 1854, only a few ships plied the waters and long stretches of the shore were uninhabited. Icy winds whipped the water's surface and hidden rocks and sandbars lurked underwater. To sea merchants such as Captain Hackett, a winter storm on such a massive body of water could be just as dangerous as a storm on the Atlantic.

On board the *Conductor*, a massive shudder suddenly gripped the ship. The hull timbers groaned and cracked, audible even above the wind. The sailors screamed, grabbing desperately for handholds as the ship tilted backward into the waves. Within a few minutes, Captain Hackett, the six members of the crew, and the cook were clinging to the rigging—the masts, sails, and ropes that rose above the deck. From their high perch, they stared down at what was once their ship. The bow of the vessel stuck up like an unstable island, and the hull disappeared beneath the waves. Every few minutes, an especially large wave would crash over the remains of the deck, spraying the sailors with icy water.

Captain Hackett was relieved to find himself alive, but he cursed himself and the weather for driving the ship aground on one of the lake's shallow sandbars. Although they had temporarily escaped drowning, it wasn't likely that he and his crew would survive for long. Through the darkness, he could just see the dim outline of a point, but there were no signs of life. He shivered inside his overcoat. Barely anyone lived along these forested shores. If he tried to swim, the waves would likely wash him away. And even if he reached land, he would be soaking wet, freezing, and alone. Better to die in the rigging than die in the waves, he decided, and gripped the ropes more tightly.

Alone on an Island

Long Point was not a point at all, as Captain Hackett had thought, but a large island—a lonely, almost deserted island partway between the American and Canadian sides of Lake Erie. Its shores were a constantly shifting arrangement of sand dunes. Inland, tree roots and brush hid swampy lakes and sucking mud. In the summer, an occasional ship stopped to trade or to pick up fresh water. In the winter, the ice and snow pressed against the beaches, cutting off all communication.

There was almost no one there, anyway. On the eastern tip, a lighthouse warned ships away from the treacherous sandbars and a single lighthouse keeper kept watch. On the entire rest of the island, there was only one dilapidated shanty—the home of trapper John Becker. And on November 24, 1854, the night the *Conductor* ran aground, John Becker was away from home.

Left on their own in the shanty were John Becker's six children and their stepmother, 26-year-old Abigail Becker. Tall and large-boned, Abigail had grown up on a farm and was already used to hard work when she married John and suddenly became a mother to his children. And after several years of marriage, she was used to fending for herself when her husband was away on trapping and hunting trips on the far side of the island. Abigail was more than capable of hauling fresh water to the cabin, chopping wood for the fire, and preparing the muskrat skins her husband would later sell to passing ships—his only access to the markets.

So despite the gale, she was up at dawn on November 25, ready to fetch water from the shore. But only a few steps from the shanty, she heard the unmistakable sound of sails snapping in the wind. Heading back inside, she sent her oldest stepson, a teenager named Edward, to investigate.

Edward headed down the beach until he could see the outlines of the ship, half sunk on a sandbar offshore. Among the ropes and the masts, he could see the bundled shapes of men. They didn't seem to be moving.

They might be still alive, but they would certainly die if they didn't get to shore, he reported to Abigail.

Abigail didn't have a boat, so if the sailors were going to reach shore, they were going to have to swim. To encourage them, she instructed the children to build a raging bonfire on the beach. She hung a kettle to boil water for tea. Then she waded into the waves, holding out her arms and beckoning to the sailors. She shouted, but the wind whipped her words away.

"If I Live..."

Captain Hackett struggled to move his fingers. After a night being soaked by the waves and sleet, they seemed frozen to the ropes. He wasn't going to survive much longer on the ship. The sight of the fire and the beckoning woman on shore had filled him with hope. Yet as he looked toward her, he also saw the channel of surging waves in his path. Would he survive the swim?

Hoping the wind would calm, the captain waited a few more hours. His men were growing steadily colder. Most had stopped talking. They all stared at the tempting bonfire.

"I will try," Captain Hackett said finally to his crew. "If I live, follow me; if I drown, stay where you are."

With that, he stripped off his boots and his frozen overcoat and jumped into the water. His muscles were stiff from the cold and the first wave crashed over his head, leaving him sputtering. Yet he forced himself to the surface and began to swim toward the shore. The waves seemed to push him forward then draw him back, but slowly the fire grew closer. He was nearly there.

Suddenly, a large wave hit the beach, then swept back toward the lake, taking Captain Hackett with it. He no longer had the strength to fight the undertow.

Seeing that he was in trouble, Abigail leaped into the water, churning forward until she was almost chest deep in the waves. The wind lashed her hair across her face and sent icy sprays of water over her head. By the time she reached the captain, his muscles were almost too stiff to move. Without pausing to wonder how she was going to drag him all the way to shore, she grabbed him by the arm and heaved with all her strength. A better grip, and then another pull. Slowly, she managed to haul him into shallower water, where they could both find safe footing. He leaned heavily on her as, with the children's help, they staggered toward the fire.

One of the shipwrecked men was safe, but it had taken all of Abigail's strength. An unexpected wave or a slip on the rocks and he could easily have been pulled back to the open water. Now soaked through and freezing herself, would Abigail have the strength to help the remaining men?

There was little time to wonder—once they saw that the captain was safely by the fire, the crew was eager to leap into the waves. After all, even a slim chance of rescue was better than the thought of freezing to death in the ropes.

The first mate was the second person to attempt the swim, but the wind quickly pushed him off course and he was carried down the shore. When Edward rushed into the water to help, a bad leg made him lose his balance, and both men were soon in trouble. Again, Abigail plowed into the lake. Clinging together, the three pulled themselves back to safety.

One by one, the rest of the sailors jumped, and swam. At least two of them lost consciousness before they reached the shore, either overcome by exhaustion or choked by water. But with the help of the children, Abigail managed to pull every one of them to the fire.

By dusk, almost a day since the ship had struck the sandbar, the captain and all six sailors were on shore. Only the cook remained in the rigging, unable to swim. There was no way to save him that night, with darkness falling and the waves still crashing. Determined to do everything she could for the sailors who had made it, Abigail took off her shawl and her shoes. Giving them to a sailor, she escorted him into the shanty. She then returned with the shawl and the shoes for the next, and the next, until she had them all inside.

Left to Die

From on board the *Conductor*, the cook saw the rest of the crew safely crowded around the fire and knew that he was going to die alone on the boat. He could barely feel his hands or his feet. Desperately, he tied himself into the ropes. If he lost consciousness, at least he wouldn't fall into the waves.

At one point, only half-conscious, he thought he saw a boat coming to his rescue. He struggled to call out for help.

Inside the shanty, Abigail had sat awake all night, tortured by thoughts of the freezing man still in the rigging. At the first sign of dawn, she woke her family and the sailors and begged them to think of some way to rescue the cook.

Outside, the group was relieved to see the man still in the ropes, and the wind a little calmer than it had been the day before. They scavenged boards that had washed ashore from the wreck and tied them together to form a crude raft. With this, they were able to paddle out to the ship. They found the cook incoherent and almost unconscious. They had to untie him from the frozen ropes, balance him on the boards, and swim, push, and kick the raft toward shore.

Hours later, when he awoke, the cook found himself safe inside with his feet soaking in a bowl of cold water—Abigail's only remedy for frostbite. It took him several weeks to fully recover, but he was eventually able to walk again.

The Story Spreads

Once the sailors were safe, they were eager to get off the island before the winter ice closed in around them. They managed to signal a passing ship, again leaving the Becker family to their solitude.

Not many people would have heard of Abigail if not for a retired sailing captain named E.P. Dorr of Buffalo, New York. He was visiting friends in Canada that winter when he heard the story of a woman on Long Point who had rescued a crew of stranded sailors. Intrigued, Dorr hired a sleigh and crossed the ice to the island to meet the woman himself. When he asked her about the rescue, she said, "I don't know as I did more 'n I ought to, nor more 'n I'd do again."

Dorr was so impressed by her actions and her humility that when he returned home, he sent a box of shoes, stockings, and clothes to her family—supplies that arrived on one of the trade ships traveling the lake in the spring. Dorr later published an account of his trip in a newspaper, and the story began to draw attention. When government officials in Ontario read it, they granted Abigail 100 acres of land on the Canadian side of Lake Erie. She also received a letter from Queen Victoria and medals from the Canadian Governor-General and the Life-Saving Benevolent Association of New York. According to one story, society members in Boston took up a collection and sent her $1000.

Although happy to receive the gifts, Abigail's family knew little of her fame. In fact, it wasn't until her stepdaughter was grown and married that she learned someone had written a newspaper article about her stepmother's achievements. Disturbed by some mistakes in the article, the stepdaughter wrote her own book about the rescue: *The Story of Abigail Becker, the Heroine of Long Point*. It was published in 1899.

According to her stepdaughter, Abigail never received the money from Boston. She was given $535 by the sailors and merchants of Buffalo, New York, and she used that money to buy a farm, a team of oxen, several small animals, and two cows. Though the first of her cows died from eating poisonous sap, and the other was killed by a falling log, Abigail spun and wove wool until she earned enough to buy a third. With her children, she managed to plow some of the fields, plant and harvest potatoes and vegetables, and cut enough wood to heat the farmhouse for the winter. Her husband preferred trapping to farming, so he went back to Long Point. He was found there after a harsh winter storm that year, frozen to death in the woods.

Abigail remarried twice, raising a total of 17 children. At 70, she was still tending her own vegetable garden. She died on March 21, 1905, at the age of 77.

Undercover Hero

Kigali, Rwanda, 1994

MARK DOYLE SAT IN THE PASSENGER SEAT as the young soldier next to him steered the United Nations car through the shattered streets of Kigali, the capital city of Rwanda in central Africa. Rwanda was the most densely populated country on the continent, and the ramshackle shops that lined Kigali's streets would have been doing booming trade on a normal day. But Mark saw barely any movement.

Lying here and there on the road, like forgotten pieces of luggage, were bodies—men, women, and children killed in the past few days of fighting. Dogs slunk among them and flies swarmed above. On the hillside that rose behind the street, a smudge of gray-brown smoke marked where a missile had hit someone's home.

On April 6, 1994, the plane of Rwandan president Habyarimana had been shot down while attempting to land at the Kigali airport. Instantly, the country had erupted into violence. The Hutu people—who made up the majority of Rwanda's population—blamed the assassination on a minority ethnic group, the Tutsis. Soon, young Hutus were attacking Tutsis throughout the city, beginning a massacre that would spread across the country and last more than three months.

Mark was a British journalist, and he gazed around intently, trying to memorize everything he saw. When the violence began, outside governments had sent planes and helicopters to evacuate their citizens, and many journalists had chosen to leave. As one of the few remaining observers, Mark felt a responsibility to tell the world what the situation was really like.

Suddenly, the car slowed to a halt. They had arrived at a Hutu checkpoint.

These checkpoints were particularly dangerous for a white man like Mark. Rwanda had been colonized and controlled by Belgium from the time of World War I until 1962, and many Rwandans still resented Belgian people. To make matters worse, Belgium had been one of the only countries willing to supply a large number of peacekeepers in 1992 when the United Nations stepped in to uphold a ceasefire agreement between the Hutus and the Tutsis. Now, these former colonists who were disliked, even hated, were supposed to be helping keep the peace.

Thinking Mark must be one of the Belgian United Nations soldiers posted in Kigali, the guard at the checkpoint poked a grenade under his nose.

"Are you Belgian?" he asked.

The young soldier driving the car spoke up. "Hey, talk to me," he told the guard. "I'm the one in charge here."

"Is that man Belgian?" the guard growled again.

"Don't be stupid," said the soldier. Then he smiled a wide, toothy smile at the guard. "I'm the only Belgian here. See? Black Belgian." He pointed to his skin and his uniform and laughed.

The soldier driving the car was Captain Mbaye Diagne, a United Nations observer from Senegal, working with the peace-keepers. When he made fun of his own position as a black man serving with the mostly white forces, the guard chuckled and waved the car through the checkpoint without further questions.

Mark breathed a shaky sigh. It was possible that Mbaye had just saved his life. There were no objective police forces left in

Kigali and barely any foreigners. If the guard had decided to kill him, his name would have simply been added to a long list of victims.

But as he shook off his fear, Mark realized that he had also witnessed something that had become legend in Kigali over the past few weeks—the smooth-talking, soldier-charming ways of Mbaye.

Disobeying Orders

Mbaye grew up in a poor Muslim family on the outskirts of Dakar, Senegal's capital city. He and his eight brothers and sisters lived in a small wooden house, bordered by narrow, dusty streets. Unlike many of the neighborhood's children, Mbaye dedicated himself to his schoolwork and became the first member of his family ever to attend university. When he graduated, he joined the Senegalese army and soon rose in the ranks. In 1993, he was sent with his troopmates to join the United Nations peacekeeping force in Rwanda.

The conflict between Rwanda's Hutu and Tutsi ethnic groups had begun before Mbaye was born. When Belgium still ruled over Rwanda, officials trained members of the small Tutsi upper class to take high government positions. Then, if any lower-class Hutus complained about laws or leadership, the Belgians could stay out of trouble by blaming the Tutsi leaders. When Belgium finally relinquished control of the country in 1962, the Hutus seized power, eager to take revenge for past wrongs.

Tutsis who had fled to the neighboring country of Uganda organized the Rwandanese Patriotic Front and invaded Rwanda in 1990, hoping to once again take power. And both Hutus and Tutsis who had managed to live peacefully in the cities and towns of Rwanda began getting caught in the crossfire. Finally, after almost three years of fighting, negotiators from other countries helped to convince the two sides to sign a ceasefire agreement and share the leadership of the country.

Like the Belgian peacekeepers, Mbaye became part of a United Nations team ordered to help maintain the ceasefire. The team was led by Major General Romeo Dallaire, a Canadian soldier on his first U.N. mission. From the start, the operation ran into trouble. When the 300 army vehicles arrived from various donor countries, 220 were broken down. No spare parts or mechanics were provided. Dallaire estimated that he would need $220 million to keep the peace in Rwanda. The U.N. gave him $54 million. He asked for 4500 soldiers, and the U.N. sent less than half that number. Worse, many of the soldiers were poorly trained and badly equipped. Bangladeshi radio technicians, for example, showed up without radios.

When the president was assassinated on April 6, 1994, the U.N. peacekeeping forces were badly informed, badly prepared, and badly organized. They scurried to find out what was going on, even as young Hutu men banded together into "death squads" and began killing Tutsis. Men, women, and children were hauled into the streets and shot or hacked to death.

The U.S. decided to evacuate all of its citizens from the country, as did other Western nations. Meanwhile, U.N. headquarters ordered Dallaire not to interfere with the conflict—his role was only to observe.

What Mbaye "observed" on the night of April 6 and the morning of April 7 was death. Thousands of Tutsi people were being mowed down, killed by the militia soldiers and by their Hutu neighbors. A radio station urged the Hutus to rid the country of Tutsi "cockroaches." Soon, corpses lay strewn on the roads and piled outside the hospitals.

Mbaye was sent to the home of Prime Minister Agathe Uwilingiyimana at 2 a.m. the morning of April 7 to protect her from the rampaging militia soldiers. He and the other peacekeepers were hassled at checkpoints and shot at before they arrived at the prime minister's house—just in time to see the prime minister and her husband hauled into the street and beaten to death.

Without thinking of his orders not to intervene, Mbaye immediately began searching for the prime minister's five children. At 2 a.m., they couldn't possibly be far away. He found them at a neighbor's house and he pressed them into a closet until the beatings outside were over.

As soon as the coast was clear, he radioed for help evacuating the children. The children cried softly from inside the closet as shots continued to ring out from nearby houses. And help didn't arrive. Finally, Mbaye decided he couldn't wait. If they stayed inside the house, the death squads outside would eventually find and kill them. He herded the children out of the closet, loaded them into a civilian's car, and drove to his own quarters in a local hotel, where he sheltered them for several hours before finding a driver to take them to safety.

Only the Beginning

The first night of violence turned into a day of killings, then a week. By the end of April 7, there were 8000 people dead. By April 11, there were 32,000. And by April 15, that number had doubled.

For the U.N. forces, the situation continued to grow worse. Belgian soldiers were taken hostage and executed by the Hutu militia. Others tried to continue peace negotiations with the Hutu and Tutsi leaders, but they had little power and no outside support from the U.N.—they could do nothing but talk.

Mbaye was assigned as a liaison between the U.N. and the Hutu army, driving back and forth between the Hotel Milles Collines, where the U.N. had set up headquarters, and the Hutu general's base. It was an incredibly dangerous position: along his route, he had to pass through 23 Hutu militia checkpoints. Mbaye knew he had to find some way to pass through those checkpoints safely. And the only way he could think of was to make friends with each and every guard on the route.

To those at the U.N. headquarters at Hotel Milles Collines, he seemed to be constantly busy, a tall, striking man striding through the lobby with notes and maps tucked under his arm. But Mbaye made sure he was never too busy to stop at a roadblock. Unlike other U.N. soldiers, who pressed their way through as quickly as possible, Mbaye often climbed out of his car to chat with the guards. He'd tease them about something until they'd break down and laugh. Or he'd harass them until they shared a cigarette with him.

One of the United Nations aid workers, Gregory "Gromo" Alex, described Mbaye's charm this way:

> Even in all this gore and hatred, as long as you can have that brief glimpse of a smile or something to laugh about that's good, you grab onto it. And with Mbaye, I think that's what everybody did. At all those checkpoints, they all knew him.

SOON, EVERYONE SEEMED TO RECOGNIZE Mbaye. On days when he didn't have time to chat, they might even wave his vehicle through.

As he smiled his thanks to his "friends" at the checkpoints, Mbaye made sure he always looked relaxed and happy to see everyone. Yet he knew that his carefree image was really a matter of life and death, because all the while Mbaye was smiling and joking and making friends, he was hiding a secret. He was single-handedly smuggling Tutsi survivors out of Kigali in the back of his Jeep.

Led by tips from neighbors or sympathetic Hutus, Mbaye would veer off his route between the U.N. and army headquarters, and navigate to an abandoned house or a dark basement to find a married couple, or a woman alone, or a pair of children hiding from the Hutus. He would then load them into his Jeep and charm his way through all 23 checkpoints back to the hotel.

Once, Mbaye found a group of 25 Tutsis hiding in a house right in the middle of the violence. There was no way to hide so many people, so Mbaye ferried them in five separate trips, each time carrying five Tutsis safely past the guards.

Turning a Blind Eye

Mbaye was disobeying orders on a daily basis. He was delaying his liaison duties to take wild detours in search of survivors. He was bribing Hutu guards with money and cigarettes. And he was constantly, personally, intervening in the conflict—exactly what the United Nations had ordered its peacekeepers not to do.

Did Romeo Dallaire know what Mbaye was up to? Did he notice that groups of Tutsis would appear in the back rooms of the hotel, only to disappear a few days later when Mbaye found ways to smuggle them out of the city? Dallaire later wrote an autobiography, but while he mentioned Mbaye as a skilled and helpful soldier, he never mentioned any undercover activities. Some of the soldiers who were in Rwanda believe that Dallaire did know, but he turned a blind eye because Mbaye was saving Tutsis, exactly what Dallaire would have liked to be doing himself.

It's also possible that Dallaire ignored these activities because Mbaye's skills were useful to the U.N. The British journalist Mark Doyle once saw a list of Rwandan people who had been working for the U.N. before the war. Some were helping feed or house the soldiers; others were working as nurses or aides for the health agencies. On the list that Mark saw, some names had lines drawn across them, showing that the workers were dead. But other names had numbers scribbled next to them. Those were the names of workers that Mbaye had saved from Hutu roadblocks. He had negotiated for their release or bribed the guards. Thirty dollars for one man's life, thirty-five for another's.

Having seen the list and having seen Mbaye herding groups of people in and out of the hotel, Mark had a suspicion that Mbaye was smuggling Tutsis away from danger. He chose not to investigate. He knew that any story he wrote about it would put Mbaye's life at risk and would stop the young soldier's single-handed rescue missions.

And more rescue missions were needed. By April 19, two weeks after the violence began, 100,000 people had been killed. Human Rights Watch declared it a genocide—the murder of an entire ethnic group. By April 25, the U.N. had voted to withdraw almost all of its peacekeepers, leaving Dallaire with only 450 soldiers. At that point, the death toll was at 144,000.

On the Front Lines

Along with his work behind the scenes, Mbaye showed courage on the front lines. At one point, the U.N. arranged to exchange Tutsis trapped at the Hotel Mille Collines with Hutus trapped behind the lines of the Tutsi rebel forces.

Mbaye was one of the soldiers ordered to protect the Tutsi refugees as they huddled in the back of an army truck for the journey out of the city. Almost as soon as the truck pulled out of the hotel gates, Hutu soldiers attacked. They had changed their minds and decided the exchange of people was unfair. Soon, men and boys waving machetes were trying to scramble into the truck.

Mbaye was unarmed but undaunted. He shouted at the attackers. He kicked and stomped their hands as they tried to climb aboard. He swung his bag at their heads, fighting them off until the truck could turn around and regain the safety of the hotel gates. In the end, the refugees waited several more weeks until they could be safely moved.

A Tragic End

On May 23, Alain Destexhe, the secretary-general of the aid group Médicins Sans Frontières, wrote a letter to the editor of the *New York Times,* begging for help from the international community. He wrote:

> Death squads and militias, originally the youth wings of the government party and its associates, armed and trained by senior government officials, are pursuing everyone perceived as opponents, and by extension this means all members of the Tutsi minority.

ACCORDING TO DESTEXHE, 200,000 Rwandans had been killed in just over a month. Half a million more were refugees, and 4000 people fled the country every day. He raged at the U.N. for its failure to help.

Still, the U.N. did nothing. And though Mbaye had saved hundreds of lives by that time, even he couldn't save the entire country by himself. He was driving alone on May 31, 1994, when a Tutsi mortar shell missed the checkpoint it was intended to strike, and hit Mbaye's Jeep instead. He was killed instantly.

The killings continued until July, when Tutsi rebels finally managed to overthrow the government and take control of Kigali. By that time, 800,000 Rwandans were dead.

For the next decade, politicians, journalists, and activists from around the world would argue about who was responsible for the massacres and who should have stepped in to stop the violence. There were no answers. And there were no answers to the question of why the entire United Nations could save so few people, when one man acting alone had saved so many.

Five Dark Days

Stockton, Utah, September 1989

TEN-YEAR-OLD JOSH DENNIS RAN his tongue over his lips. His mouth was completely dry, as if it had been stuffed full of cotton balls. He thought about the meals at his elementary school cafeteria and pictured one of the hamburgers they served for lunch. It seemed so real and so delicious that he could smell it. He could almost see it floating in the darkness.

But when he blinked, he couldn't see anything. This wasn't the kind of darkness that filled his bedroom at night. In his room, he could still see the silhouette of the doorway and the shadows of the furniture. Here, it was so dark that opening his eyes or closing them made no difference at all. He couldn't see his hands when he held them in the air. How long had he been trapped? One day? Two? He had no way of knowing.

JOSH HAD BEEN TOO YOUNG to go on the Boy Scout camping trip to Hidden Treasure Mine in the ghost town of Stockton, Utah. But his dad, Terry, was the troop leader and had bent the rules for him. When the boys had collected their gear and reviewed their safety rules that Friday evening, the trip had seemed like a huge adventure. The abandoned mine had six levels and stretched for more than 12 kilometers (8 miles) into the mountainside. In the 1880s, miners had carved lead, copper, silver, and zinc out of the stone, but now the shafts stood open and deserted, one lonely

NO TRESPASSING sign waving near the entrance—a sign that scouts and amateur explorers regularly ignored.

It was after dinner when Josh set out with his dad and three other boys. Long, dark passageways seemed to extend in every direction and the flashlights cast eerie circles of light on the hewn rock walls. The boys loved the way their voices echoed in the chambers and they shouted back and forth with a larger group ahead of them. But soon one of the scouts, a visually impaired boy a few years older than Josh, became disoriented and scared. Josh's dad volunteered to lead him back out of the mine.

"Do you want to come?" Terry asked Josh.

When Josh shook his head, Terry agreed to let him go with the two older boys for a few minutes until they caught up with the large group in the tunnel ahead. There were several guides with that group, and he knew the addition of a few more boys wouldn't be a problem. Josh watched his dad's flashlight beam light the path out.

Then he turned back toward the older boys, Cary and Tyler, ready to explore more of the mine. But Cary and Tyler hadn't realized he was planning to stay with them—they'd moved ahead, and their flashlight beams were circles of light already far down the shaft. Josh turned again. His dad's flashlight beam had disappeared around a corner.

Deciding to head for the lights he could see, Josh hurried after the two older boys. They were speeding up, trying to catch the larger group, and Josh had to jog to keep them in sight, dodging puddles and tripping on rocks as he went. Then they turned a corner.

Josh stopped dead. It was suddenly pitch black, as if he had been locked in a closet. The mine seemed colder and scarier without light, but he tried to stay calm. There was no reason to worry, he told himself, but it wouldn't be safe to try to follow Cary and Tyler when he didn't know which direction they were heading. So he turned, reached out his hand to touch the wall on his right, and began to follow his dad's path to safety.

Within a few minutes, Josh knew he was lost. He could no longer hear the other Boy Scouts, and he couldn't see any exit ahead. He was disoriented in the dark. Had they turned right or left on the way in? He couldn't remember. He stumbled into another puddle and the chilled water soaked through his shoes.

The shaft seemed to be leading him uphill, but there was still no light and no sign of an exit. Josh knew he was completely lost. There was nothing to do except wait. Shivering, he sank down onto the rock floor and said a prayer that someone would find him quickly.

Where's Josh?

Cary and Tyler emerged from the mine shaft, blinking in the evening light.

"Where's Josh?" asked Terry.

They looked at him in surprise. They had thought Josh left the mine with his dad when Terry led the other boy back to the exit.

Feeling a knot of worry form in his stomach, Terry posted himself by the mine's entrance and began stopping each group of scouts.

"Did you see Josh in there?"

"Was Josh with you?"

It was 9:30 p.m. No one had seen Josh in hours, and it was growing dark outside. The Scout leaders donned their ropes and gear and headed back into the mine. Some of them were expert climbers and cavers. They would have no problem finding Josh, especially as he hadn't been far into the mine when he and Terry had separated.

They split up, heading down the nearest shafts and shouting Josh's name. Again and again, they called for him, gradually working their way deeper into the mine. Five hours later, they had found nothing. One of the leaders, Ray Van Sleeuwen, felt as if he had been so alert to sounds that he would have heard the smallest noise. He hiked and hiked through the shafts, trying to stay hopeful that Josh was just around the next corner, or just through the next opening. Every time a cavern proved empty, it hurt even more.

At 2:30 a.m., they contacted the Tooele County sheriff, who called out the local search and rescue team. There were hundreds of mines in the area, some left over from the gold rush of the 19th century and some still in operation. The search and rescue members were experienced climbers and rappellers—if there was a boy lost in Hidden Treasure Mine, they were confident that they could find him. They broke into teams, marking their paths with ribbons so that they could cross off each section of the mine as they searched it.

Within a few hours, the teams were joined by search dogs. Outside the mine, each dog sniffed Josh's pillow, then set off to find his scent. Soon, a dog barked at a shaft opening outside the main mine—Josh had been exploring near there before he joined his dad's group inside. Another dog barked at a second shaft—this one filled with poisonous gases. Josh had also been standing near this one before entering the mine. The searchers led the dogs inside the main shaft. But because there was no ventilation, there were no breezes to carry Josh's scent. The hard rock floors of the tunnels gave few clues.

The county search and rescue members worked through the night. By morning, there was still no sign of Josh.

Desperate Efforts

Josh's mom, Janeen, had arrived in Stockton after hearing that her son was missing. Now she paced back and forth in a nearby hotel room, waiting for news.

She wasn't the only one to arrive when news spread that a boy was lost in the mine. Members of the family's church came to volunteer, a local construction company owner bought his entire staff new pairs of boots and sent them to help, and Utah Power and Light sent its rescue team, trained in mine fires and emergencies. Miners who had worked in the shafts years before also turned up to help. There were now 200 volunteers searching the area.

They explored every shaft, cavern, and vent that they could find. Some donned oxygen masks and lowered themselves into gas-filled chambers. Some scoured the more than 200 air vents outside. Two helicopters swooped over the surrounding woods in case Josh had found his own way out.

By the end of the second day, they were sure that they had covered the entire mine. Every wall inside was marked with colored ribbons to show that searchers had passed through. The sheriff's staff was convinced that Josh must have left the mine and gotten lost in the surrounding hills. They moved their search above ground.

"We've been through the whole mine, every square inch of it, three times and he's not there," the sheriff's dispatcher told reporters.

Josh's mom wasn't so sure. Janeen had a feeling that Josh would have climbed, that he was somewhere high. She told her hunch to the officials, but they assured her that they had searched everywhere a small boy could have reached in the dark. He was not inside the mine.

One Man's Memories

John Skinner had grown up near Hidden Treasure Mine, and he'd ventured inside to explore the passages when he was about 10 years old, the same age as Josh. Once he'd experienced the excitement of walking the deserted historic shafts, he'd gone back more than 100 times. All his life, he had felt connected to the mine. After all, his father, his grandfather, and his great-grandfather had all worked there. Now, John was in the midst of writing about the mine's history.

When he returned from a vacation to discover that a 10-year-old boy had been lost inside for two days, John felt compelled to help. He climbed in his car on Sunday morning and drove up toward the entrance. Soon he was stopped at a roadblock. The area was closed because of an ongoing search, the official told him. He would have to turn back.

John explained that he was going to volunteer to join the search, but the official assured him that there were more than enough people already searching. He would have to return home.

Instead of following instructions, John decided to try another, riskier, tactic. He would drive to the entrance of Buckhorn Mine, which wound through from the other side of the mountain to eventually connect to the Hidden Treasure Mine shafts. That way, no officials could stop him. But as John hiked through the tunnels of Buckhorn Mine, he could see they were unsafe. The beams were falling and some of the tunnels were caving in. Rocks tumbled down the walls as he moved through.

There was no sense continuing if he was going to get trapped inside and become another target for the search teams. Frustrated, John retraced his steps and returned home. But he couldn't stop thinking about the boy. That night, he kept waking his wife to talk about the rescue efforts.

On Monday morning, John returned to the roadblock and tried to persuade the sheriff to let him through. The sheriff was firm—200 searchers were more than enough. He couldn't have amateur historians running through the mine, causing more confusion.

Again, John returned home.

A Last Try

They have all the searchers they need, John told himself. If Josh is there, the searchers will find him. All day Tuesday, he tried to put the situation out of his mind. The local newspaper headlines didn't help. "Hope Fading Fast for Boy Lost 4 Days. Searchers Now Battling Fatigue, Despair," they read. The more John tried not to think about it, the more he worried. There had to be a way to help.

On Wednesday, as the newspaper reported that the search was winding down and hope of finding Josh alive was virtually gone, John was still worrying. He even spent his lunch hour in a diner scribbling a map of the cave onto a paper napkin, and trying to imagine places where he thought a small boy could get lost. There were three main spots, and he marked each with an X.

After lunch, with his map in hand, he couldn't resist trying to get to the mine one more time. He drove a back route up the mountain, taking seldom-used roads to avoid the sheriff and the roadblock.

Finally, he succeeded. He got near the mine's entrance and

managed to persuade some of the Utah Power and Light searchers that he could help. After all, he told them, they had tried everything else. What did they have to lose by letting him check a few places in the mine? He showed them his napkin, where he had marked the three possible spots.

Still skeptical, but willing to try anything, 18 searchers followed John into the shaft. Two of the most hopeful searchers were Ray Guyman, who was deaf in one ear, and Gary Christensen. As they entered the shafts for what felt like the hundredth time, Gary turned to his friend and said, "We can't stop. I just know we can't stop. Our job's not done yet."

They hiked directly toward the first X on John's map—a place where fallen beams had created a hole in the tunnel that a confused boy might have wandered through. But Josh wasn't there. He wasn't in the second place, either.

After about 20 minutes, John's group of searchers began to split up. Only Gary and Ray stayed with him. They hiked toward the third X on John's map, a dead end where a large pocket of ore had been hollowed out by miners.

They swept their lights around the chamber. Nothing.

Suddenly Ray called for them to stop. "I think I hear something," he said.

Both John and Gary raised skeptical eyebrows. They knew Ray was half deaf. But they stopped and listened. And heard a faint sound, so soft that it would have easily been blocked out by the tramping of their boots.

"Keep yelling!" John called.

And they began to hear it more clearly. It was coming from above them.

Gary began scrambling frantically up the sloped side of the chamber, calling for Josh to slide down. Hidden high on the wall of the large chamber was a tiny, almost invisible opening. They had found Josh—trapped in a small hollowed-out pocket about 2 meters (6 feet) wide and 9 meters (30 feet) deep. The pocket was so small and the entrance to it so shadowed that searchers had passed by six times without seeing it. Only from directly beside it was the space visible at all. Josh had wandered up several levels, until he was 150 meters (500 feet) above where he and his dad had separated. Thick rock walls had muffled the sounds of his shouting.

Overwhelmed, Gary grabbed Josh in a bear hug. "We're going to take you to your mom and dad," he said.

"My dad's outside," Josh told them, "but my mom's at home." He had no idea that he had been trapped inside for five days, more than enough time for his mom and hundreds of other worried searchers to gather.

A Miraculous Recovery

Josh was rushed to a children's hospital, where doctors treated him for dehydration, exhaustion, and frostbite. After a few weeks in a wheelchair, he was back on his feet. In a few months, he was skateboarding again.

Josh's rescue was hailed across the country as a miracle. He had survived alone in the dark for five days with no water and only a package of candy for food. There were newspaper and television interviews, church appearances, and speeches. Even President George Bush sent him a letter: "I am so happy to hear that you were found safe and unharmed.... Your experience is testimony that miracles do happen."

To Josh, it all seemed overwhelming. He just wanted to go back to his regular life.

Years later, he told a newspaper reporter that faith and positive thinking got him through the experience.

"I didn't know the mine had tons of mine shafts that drop for hundreds of feet, or that people supposedly could survive without water for about three days before they died of dehydration," he said. "I think that's one of the things that definitely preserved my life. I didn't focus on those types of things."

Doctors later guessed that by sleeping and staying still, Josh had slowed his metabolism and managed to stay alive on the ledge, confident that he would be rescued. And he was. For the searchers, and for Josh, it was as if five days of hopes and prayers had suddenly been answered.

Entombed Underwater

The Atlantic Ocean near Portsmouth, New Hampshire, May 23, 1939

"RIG FOR DIVE," called Captain Naquin. Throughout the sub, men hurried to their positions, sealing hatches and checking pressure valves as they went.

The USS *Squalus* was one of the American navy's newest submarines. About 92 meters (300 feet) long and 8 meters (27 feet) wide, the vessel was the same dark gray as the Atlantic waters and could slide along the surface about as fast as a car could drive through city streets.

Inside the steel hull, 4 officers and 51 submariners worked as smoothly as the newly tuned engines, each man responsible for specific duties before, during, and after each dive. They had already completed 18 successful test dives and the *Squalus* was almost ready to officially join the navy fleet. Today, they would attempt an emergency battle descent. Imagining that an enemy ship was bearing down on them, they would plunge the nose of the sub into the water, diving 15 meters (50 feet) in less than a minute. For today's nuclear-powered submarines, such a dive would be routine. But in the 1930s, diesel-powered engines and the need to rely on battery power made diving slower and more dangerous.

Although World War II wouldn't start until August 1939 and the United States wouldn't declare war until 1941, the newspapers carried plenty of stories about conflicts in Europe. And most of the submariners had family members or friends who had fought in World War I. Peering out over the choppy waters, with the cliffs of the coastline fading from sight and dark clouds bearing down from the sky, it wasn't hard to imagine they were about to join a real battle, or a real war.

Naval architect Harold Preble took his position by the chart desk in the control room. He checked the pressure valves and controls that were his responsibility, then glanced around the room. Everything was ready.

It was 8:30 a.m.

"Stand by to dive!" called Captain Naquin.

The first alarm rang out to warn the crew.

The diesel engines stopped and tanks in the front of the submarine were flooded to pull the nose down. In the control room, Harold watched as the board of lights that connected all parts of the ship flashed green. The men called the board the "Christmas Tree," and when the lights went green, the vessel was ready to dive.

The second alarm clanged. More tanks were flooded.

In 62 seconds—slightly longer than Captain Naquin had hoped—the *Squalus* sank to 15 meters (50 feet).

One of the valves needed to be adjusted, so Harold edged himself along the side of the chart table and reached up to turn the handle.

Suddenly a blast of pressure struck him, as if he had been hit by a wall of air. A split second later, a ventilation line above him burst. Water spewed out in all directions, knocking down another crew member, who fell on Harold, carrying them both to the floor.

Unable to move, Harold watched as water poured through

the doors at either end of the control room. Other crew members struggled to force the hatches closed.

The lights went out.

Harold felt the ship tilt, then tilt more steeply as it slid down through the water. With an echoing clunk, the *Squalus* hit the ocean floor, 74 meters (243 feet) below the waves.

A Call to Action

Charles "Swede" Momsen was running tests that day in the Experimental Diving Unit of the navy yard in Washington, D.C. The 43-year-old lieutenant commander had earned his nickname in navy training for his Viking-like looks. But it was his dedication to submarine safety that had gained him fame in the navy ranks.

Fourteen years before, Swede had been a young captain thrilled about his new posting aboard the *S-1*, one of the most technologically advanced submarines in the world. He was waiting at the submarine base in New London, Connecticut, when an officer woke him in the middle of the night. One of his sister submarines, the *S-51*, had rammed a passenger ship and sunk off the coast. There was no sign of the crew. Swede immediately assembled his team and spent the next few hours combing the waters until he found an oil slick and air bubbles that marked where the unlucky sub had gone down.

A close friend of Swede's was aboard the vessel, along with many acquaintances, but there was no sign of life and no possibility of rescue. When a submarine sank, there was simply no way to get to the crew. The trapped submariners died in the dark, their oxygen slowly running out, the weight of the ocean pressing down on them and sealing the hatches shut.

Of course, even if the trapped submariners aboard the *S-51* had somehow managed to open the hatches, they would have been crushed by the rush of incoming water. And if they had survived that, they would have died of the bends.

"The bends" is the common name for decompression sickness. Under pressure, nitrogen in the air will dissolve into water, the same way air is trapped in an unopened bottle of cola. When divers are in deep water, some of the air from their lungs dissolves into the water in their bodies. If they rise in the water too fast, that air is released, the same way the air in the cola is released when the bottle is opened. In a human body, that sudden release of air can be fatal.

To avoid the bends, divers must either rise through the water extremely slowly, stopping along the way to allow their bodies to adjust, or else go immediately into decompression chambers, where artificial pressure tricks their bodies into thinking they are still underwater.

If the trapped submariners of the S-51 had managed to open an escape hatch, they wouldn't have been able to hold their breath for long enough to rise slowly through the water. And because rescue boats didn't know their exact location, there were no decompression chambers waiting for them on the surface.

For Swede, the deaths of his friends aboard the S-51 marked a turning point. He dedicated himself to preventing future tragedies.

Ideas under Pressure

Though he had no background in engineering, Swede managed to come up with two entirely new pieces of rescue equipment. The first was the Momsen Lung, which Swede first tested in 1929. Everyone knew it was possible to dive underwater, breathing air pumped through a hose from the surface. But no one had successfully invented an enclosed system that a diver could carry with him.

Swede's idea was this: a diver would breathe through a hose into a bag around his chest. Inside the bag, soda lime would filter out the carbon dioxide. A small supply of fresh oxygen would allow the diver to keep breathing as he swam to the surface, and would allow the bag to act as a life preserver. Today, with scuba diving so popular, the Momsen Lung seems shockingly basic. But to the navy in the 1930s, it was the first glimmer of hope that lost submariners could save themselves.

Momsen's second idea was just as revolutionary. Why, he wondered, couldn't a ship on the surface lower a large metal compartment full of air, connect the compartment to the escape hatch of a sunken submarine, then lift submariners a few at a time to the surface?

When it was built, with the help of navy engineers and several colleagues, the rescue chamber looked like a massive upside-down pear. Inside, it was split into two compartments. The larger top compartment was filled with air, and allowed divers to ride down with the chamber. In the small bottom compartment was a seal that would connect to the submarine's escape hatch, along with ballast tanks that would fill with water to help control how quickly the chamber rose and sank.

It was this rescue bell that would offer hope to the *Squalus* submariners, trapped on the ocean floor.

WHEN THE ADMIRAL AT THE NAVY BASE in Portsmouth didn't receive word from the *Squalus* after its test dive, and when other ships in the area could find no trace of the sub, Swede Momsen was the obvious man to call.

He was eating his lunch at the Washington navy yard when the phone rang. It was a navy commander with these short words: "*Squalus* is down off Isles of Shoals, depth between 200 and 400 feet. Have your divers and equipment ready to leave immediately."

Choosing two doctors and an expert diver to accompany him, Swede was on his way within the hour. More divers followed close behind, and one of the rescue chambers would meet them at the scene.

The chamber was tested in the early 1930s, but had never been used in a real emergency. When the *Squalus* sank, the closest available chamber was on board the *Falcon*, a converted minesweeper docked in New London, Connecticut, to the south. There was only one problem: the *Falcon* was being overhauled, its engines had been shut down, and the crew was on leave. The captain set every available engineer to work on the engines, while local police rounded up the crew. Within an hour, every sailor was on board, ready for duty.

Silence Undersea

On board the *Squalus*, three hours after the sub hit bottom, Harold huddled under a blanket with two other men. There were 33 survivors crowded together, trying to keep warm and trying not to think about the 26 men who had drowned in the stern compartments. In that section of the vessel, the water had poured in too quickly for the men to escape and seal the hatches.

Not knowing how they had sunk or whether they could be rescued, the men huddled together. Water weighs much more than air, and the weight of the sea pressed down on them, making their bodies feel twice as heavy as usual. The cold of the water was also seeping through the vessel. And despite the small amounts of fresh oxygen that the captain was having released from the storage tanks, the air was slowly turning foul.

Trapped underwater without power, Captain Naquin ordered

his men to release a radio wire attached to a buoy. This would allow any passing vessel to communicate with them. He also ordered the crew to fire a distress rocket. Half an hour later, he ordered another one fired. Then another. When four hours had passed, they had fired six rockets, and received no response.

To distract the men, the captain ordered some of the canned food distributed to the crew. Harold was eating peaches and pine-apple straight out of the tin when he heard something.

Chop, chop, chop.

Was he imagining it?

After each rocket had been fired, Harold and the other men had strained to hear the sound of an approaching ship. Were their ears playing tricks on them now?

But no, the sound was getting stronger. Chop, chop, chop.

The men were hearing the sounds of the *Sculpin*'s propellers. The *Squalus*'s sister submarine, the *Sculpin,* had been criss-crossing the nearby waters for what seemed like endless hours, looking for any sign of the downed vessel, when a young lookout thought he spotted a smudge of smoke on the horizon. He had seen the most recent of the *Squalus*'s signal rockets.

Inside the *Squalus*, the men gave a hopeful cheer. Captain Naquin ordered yet another rocket, and this one exploded right in front of the *Sculpin*.

Once the *Sculpin* fished the radio buoy out of the ocean, the captain was able to make radio contact. But only for a split second. Without warning, a high wave struck the *Sculpin*, stretching, then snapping, the radio cable. Contact with the *Squalus* was lost.

A few messages were sent from the *Squalus* by Morse code—a crew member pounding on the hull with as much strength as possible to hammer out a short message for the *Sculpin*. Trained to listen for underwater sounds, the technicians on the *Sculpin* squeezed their headphones to their ears and managed to decode the banging—the submariners were alive, and in the bow.

Help Arrives

Hour after hour, the *Sculpin* stood guard over the site. Nothing else could be done until help arrived. And finally, it did. A tugboat brought the navy admiral to the scene. A Coast Guard plane circled overhead, watching for any submariners who might escape to the surface. The *Brooklyn*, a massive cruiser with medical facilities, approached. (In fact, the ship had left New York City so quickly that half the crew members were still on shore.) There were also several more tugs carrying medical and salvage equipment, patrol boats to ferry crew members back and forth, and the Coast Guard cutter with Swede on board. And finally, 23 hours after the accident, the *Falcon* chugged into the area with the rescue chamber.

SWEDE HAD ONE PRESSING QUESTION when he arrived on the scene. Why hadn't the submariners used his Momsen Lungs? The *Squalus* was equipped with a full set, and most of the men on board had been trained in their use. In Swede's opinion, strong, uninjured submariners would have been able to rise to the surface without difficulty if they'd used the lung right away.

On board the sub, Captain Naquin had reached a different decision. The water below was too cold and the weather above too rough to allow the men to swim to safety. And now, almost a full day after the accident, it was too late. Too many men were weakened by oxygen deprivation and cold.

So the rescue chamber on board the *Falcon* was the submariners' last hope. To find the hatch, clear it of debris, and connect the cable that would guide the rescue chamber, Swede chose a stout diver from the *Falcon's* crew, Martin Sibitsky. Dressed in an awkward canvas diving suit (including a belt of lead to help him sink through the water) and a massive metal diving helmet, Martin wore equipment that weighed more than he did. His fellow divers connected air hoses and radio lines to his suit, allowing him to receive air and instructions from the surface. They then lowered him overboard on a diving platform.

As Martin descended into the water, the darkness growing thicker around him, Swede talked to him constantly. In 1939, they didn't have the careful mix of gases that divers breathe today. Under the intense pressure of the ocean, the gases that Martin was breathing would turn toxic, making it hard for him to move and even harder for him to think clearly. If he breathed them for too long, they could even be fatal.

He landed on the bow of the *Squalus*. With prompting from Swede, Martin found the sub's escape hatch, connected the rescue chamber's cable, and cleared some loose debris out of the way. In his "under-pressure" state, those simple tasks took 22 minutes, but he returned to the *Sculpin* successful.

On the surface, sailors took the cable that Martin had attached to the sub and attached it in turn to the rescue chamber. Two operators climbed in, and the chamber was lowered into the water, connected to the surface by the guide cable, an electrical wire, and two air hoses. Achingly slowly, the chamber sank. At last, after more than half an hour, the operators reported that the sub was in sight.

All went smoothly. First, the chamber operators blew a blast of compressed air into the bottom compartment, blowing out the water inside. Then they bolted the bottom of the chamber onto the top of the sub, and prepared to open the hatch.

Footsteps

Aboard the *Squalus*, Harold huddled under his blanket and waited. Some of the men near him had nodded off to sleep, half-drugged by the bad air. Harold stayed awake, shivering, and wondered if the rescuers would get him out alive, or if he would die trapped underwater.

He kept hoping, and his hope was kept alive by one name—Swede Momsen. The night before, the sailors on the surface had banged out a message in Morse code, telling the men below that Swede had arrived on the scene. Harold knew Swede's reputation. In fact, he'd been exchanging letters with the inventor as part of an ongoing argument. (Swede had complained that stopwatches supplied by Harold's department were inaccurate.) If anyone could save them, it would be Swede. Harold repeated the thought to himself again and again.

Almost two hours before, he was sure he had heard stomping footsteps on the hull above. But now nothing. He waited…

Thud. Something heavy struck the hull, sending vibrations through the submarine. Instantly, everyone was awake. Soon, they could hear scraping around a hatch, and they pressed close. A few minutes of silence seemed excruciatingly long. Would the rescuers be able to get in?

Finally, the hatch opened with a creak, and light and fresh air flooded into the submarine.

"Well, we're here," the chamber operator said simply. And soon he was handing down sandwiches, soup, and coffee.

Harold's first urge was to elbow his way through the crowd and leap into the rescue chamber, but like the other men he remained calm and patient, breathing in the new air with relief.

"Why the delay?" called a member of the crew.

"Where are the napkins?" joked another.

Captain Naquin selected seven submariners for the first trip to the surface, and Harold's name was on the list. Fourteen minutes after they climbed in, the *Falcon* began reeling in the cable and the chamber departed for the surface.

Harold was the second submariner to climb out of the rescue chamber and stand on the deck of the *Falcon*. He greeted Swede with a bear hug, and promised to get him new stopwatches right away.

Cranking It Up

Harold was rushed to a decompression chamber, so he wasn't on deck to see the rescue chamber bring up a second, then a third load of survivors.

As the third group of men staggered out of the chamber and into the fresh air, the sky grew darker and a few raindrops fell. It was just after 7 p.m., more than 35 hours since the submarine had gone down. There were only eight men left aboard the *Squalus*: Captain Naquin, Lieutenant Doyle, and six submariners.

John Mihalowski had operated the chamber for the first three trips, and he would take it down again. He was joined by Swede's most experienced diver, Jim McDonald. For an hour, they glided slowly down toward the ocean floor, the sea growing darker every minute. Jim bolted the chamber to the sub, and the remaining men climbed aboard. Captain Naquin was the last to leave the sunken vessel.

Within 20 minutes, the seal was released and the *Falcon* again began the long process of reeling up the chamber. Ten minutes, twenty minutes…

Suddenly the ascent stopped. Inside the chamber, the cable had jammed in the reel. And strained by the sudden pressure, the motor that ran the wheel coughed and fell silent. The chamber was stuck, only halfway to the surface.

John and Jim tried to coax the motor back to life. They tried to rewind the cable onto the reel. But nothing worked. The sudden stop had tangled the wire, and the motor refused to cooperate. There was nothing to do but lower the chamber back to the bottom of the sea.

After being so close to rescue, it was agonizing to once again descend into the darkness. But none of the submariners expressed fear or doubt. They waited patiently while Swede sent down a diver to cut the old cable free and attach a new one. But by this time, the cable, the electrical wire, and their air hoses were hopelessly tangled. Unable to sort them out, the diver returned to the surface.

Another diver went down to try to attach a new cable to the chamber, but the confusion of wires snared his air hose on the way down. By the time he freed himself, he was almost incoherent from the lack of fresh air. Swede ordered him hauled up and rushed to the decompression chamber. The diver was able to pass along one thing—the cable connecting the Falcon and the rescue chamber was worse than anyone had imagined. The piece of it that remained—the only thing that kept the chamber from becoming lost at the bottom of the sea—was a metal strand the width of a piece of string.

Despite the increasingly bad weather, a third diver was sent down. For more than half an hour, until he could no longer feel his hands, he struggled to connect a new cable. Finally, worried that the diver was close to passing out, Swede ordered him hauled to the surface.

There was only one thing left to try. Swede would instruct the operators inside the chamber to release tiny amounts of ballast water at a time. That would cause the chamber to float ever so slowly to the surface, and the Falcon could delicately pull in the damaged cable. If it worked, the submariners would soon be on the surface. If it failed, and the cable or the air hoses snapped, they would be irretrievably lost.

The weather was growing worse as Swede calmly radioed his instructions to the chamber. Blow ballast for 15 seconds, he ordered. Then 15 seconds more. Those on board the *Falcon* were so tense that not a single person spoke except for Swede. Again, 15 seconds. A fourth time.

At last, Swede felt the cable in his hands grow looser. Ten men hauled on it, drawing it carefully over the edge of the boat. Hand over hand, agonizingly slowly, they pulled the cable in. When the waves, as high as a tall man, dipped the boat down, they pulled harder. When the water lifted the *Falcon,* pulling the line tight, the men allowed slack. All they thought of was the piece of "string" connecting them to the chamber.

Swede peered through the darkness to where the cable emerged from the water, until at last he could see the place where the metal had frayed. Balanced precariously, the men held the cable while a deckhand reached a fresh strand to below the breaking point and clamped it on—the chamber was securely attached once again. With new strength, the sailors on the surface hauled again and again on the cable until finally the metal top of the chamber broke the surface of the waves. A simultaneous cheer rose from the deck.

Once the rescue chamber hatch was lifted for the last time, 39 hours after the *Squalus*'s fatal dive, Captain Naquin followed his men onto the deck of the *Falcon*. He then joined other survivors in the decompression chamber, and fell into his first real sleep since the ordeal began.

What the Future Held

At the time of the rescue, the submariners on board the *Squalus* had no idea what had caused the sinking. It wasn't until the following summer, when the submarine was recovered from the sea floor, that investigators found an open air intake valve meant to draw air when the vessel was on the surface. Either the valve malfunctioned or an operator accidentally opened it during the dive, allowing seawater to rush inside. No one would ever know for sure.

Four divers won the Medal of Honor from the United States Congress for their efforts in the rescue, including Jim McDonald and John Mihalowski, the two divers within the chamber during its fourth, near disastrous, trip.

When the men who had endured hours of near-death on the ocean floor had fully recovered from the ordeal, they were offered the postings of their choice in the navy. Every single one chose to return to duty on a submarine.

And back at the experimental diving unit, Swede was already working on more rescue techniques. He perfected a mix of helium and oxygen that would allow divers to work deep underwater without suffering from the mind-numbing effects of toxic oxygen that had hampered the divers during the *Squalus* rescue.

Soon after, Swede was transferred to Pearl Harbor and was serving there when the harbor was bombed by Japanese forces in 1942. He commanded two submarine squadrons during the war, and earned the Navy Cross for extraordinary heroism, along with two awards for merit. He rose to the rank of vice admiral before retiring in 1955.

By the time Swede died in 1967, his innovations were part of an ongoing revolution in submarine and diving technology. And today, the world's ships have access to equipment that even Swede would never have imagined.

Still, a dive will always have elements of danger. In 2000, despite rescue efforts by Russian and Norwegian teams, 118 men died on board a Russian submarine after an explosion. And in 2004, a Canadian died after a fire on board HMCS *Chicoutimi*.

Despite these tragedies, the chances of underwater rescue are greater than ever before. For instance, in August 2005 a high-tech Russian mini-sub became tangled in fishing nets in the 183-metre (600-foot) deep waters of the Pacific Ocean near the Bering Sea, with seven people trapped inside. Russian naval rescuers were able to use sonar and radio contact to locate the sub and hook it from a vessel on the surface, but couldn't tow it to shallow waters. Then U.S. and British navy teams flew to their aid with two Super Scorpios, robotic vehicles that can dive up to 1524 meters (5000 feet). Equipped with lights, sonar, and video cameras, the vessels would use their robotic arms to cut the mini-sub free of the tangled nets.

The British Super Scorpio arrived on the scene first, and was able to free the mini-sub. After three days on the bottom, dressed in thermal suits and lying as still as possible to conserve oxygen, the submariners were able to surface and open the hatch to escape.

Swede would have been proud.

Chaos under the Big Top

Hartford, Connecticut, July 6, 1944

CROWDS HAD GATHERED FOR DAYS watching the canvas of the big top rise into the air, catching glimpses of the elephants and tigers, seeing the acrobats flit in and out of the tent. When the Ringling Brothers and Barnum & Bailey Circus opened on July 6, 1944, it seemed as if every child in Hartford, Connecticut, was there.

For many, it must have been an exhilarating week. First, there had been the picnics and parties for the Fourth of July. Then an extra day off. And now the circus was in town! In the air, the smells of roasting peanuts and straw mingled with a whiff of manure. It was hot and humid and a thunderstorm threatened, but the crowd didn't care. They poured into the circus tent with eyes only for the opening parade that was circling center ring.

For about a century, this sort of circus had been touring the United States, astounding audiences with acts from all over the world. There were wild animals from Africa combined with acrobats from Russia, contortionists from India, and weight lifters from Europe. The largest shows employed more than 1000 people and required 100 double-length railcars to travel from town to town. In 1944, World War II had created a shortage of workers and financial troubles for the circus, but audiences still arrived expecting to see the "greatest show on earth."

On July 6, there were 8000 spectators crammed onto the

bleachers. From his position near the entrance, photographer Dick Miller snapped shots of children pointing and laughing as the clowns took the stage. There was a rattle behind him and he moved aside slightly as workers brought in one of the circus's steel chutes—a kind of narrow metal hallway that allowed the wild animals one by one into the tent. The chute took up part of the doorway, but it didn't block Dick's view of the center ring, where the clowns were tumbling and the lions, tigers, jaguars, and leopards were performing.

As the animals were led back to the chute, the Flying Wallendas took their place. Balancing on high wires far above the crowd, the Wallendas spun and swayed until Dick found himself holding his breath and half-closing his eyes like the children across from him.

Suddenly, something flickered at the edges of his vision. He glanced to the side to see a tiny ember of flame, like a glowing cigarette tip, spark in the canvas tent and lick its way up a support rope.

Fire!

Immediately, Dick shouted for help.

Outside, a police officer heard the shout and looked toward the canvas in time to see a glow of orange light turn into a burst of flame, exploding through the canvas and already roaring its way up the tent.

Ringmaster Fred Bradna was standing inside, not too far from Dick. When he saw the smoke, he instantly blew his whistle, the shrill sound piercing the music and cheers. He also yelled to Merle Evans, the band leader. After traveling with the circus for 26 years, Merle knew that music might help people to stay calm and keep their bearings in the smoke. He led his 29-member band in "The Stars and Stripes Forever," the traditional circus code for disaster, blasting out the notes right over the roar of the confused crowd.

When the performers heard the song, they ran for their emergency stations or headed for safety. The Flying Wallendas—the only act on stage at the time—came sliding down their guy wires and ran for the stage exits. The announcer turned on the public address system and asked the audience members to quickly leave the tent.

Inferno

The experienced leaders of the circus knew that fire was a constant danger. Just two years before the Hartford fire, flames in the animal pens had consumed the area in minutes, killing 65 animals. But there were few experienced leaders left at the Ringling Brothers and Barnum & Bailey Circus in 1944. A recent family uproar had seen the two brothers who had guided the circus removed from their positions. According to one of the brothers—John Ringling North—the entire operation was left to be run by an opera star (the son of the original Ringling Circus founder), an accountant who had never traveled with a circus, a banker, and two old women with no firsthand experience.

There was also a shortage of experienced workers. Most young men had gone off to fight in World War II and those who had stayed at home were needed in the factories or on the farms. It was almost impossible to find staff for a circus. Usually, there would be about 800 men and women scurrying around the big tent. In 1944, the operation was run by about 350.

The combination of inexperienced leaders and overworked staff led to some bad decisions. The circus abandoned its fireproof tent because of leaks, and went back to an old version—one that was watertight because it was treated with a mixture of wax and gas. During the circus, fire-fighting pumps and hoses were supposed to be loaded onto tractors and arranged at intervals around the tent. But in the scurry of the pre-performance chaos, they were never ordered into position. The fire extinguishers that were supposed to be placed under the seats in the bleachers were never even unloaded from the train.

Inside the tent, the crowd had no way to know that there was no fire-fighting equipment and no hope of rescue. As the air grew hotter, people could see the flames roaring 30 meters (100 feet) above them, at the top of the tent. Pieces of burning canvas began raining down and the chaos on the floor of the tent grew worse. Soon, they were surrounded by an immense wall of burning canvas, trapped in a circle of fire.

In panic, people began pushing and shoving against one another until some were being crushed in the crowd. Mothers lost their grip on their children and turned back, trying to press against the tide of people. In the reserved rows on the floor, people pushed their folding chairs out of the way, then tripped on the fallen chairs of other people.

At the main entrance, employees were trying to guide people, but they too were being crushed by the crowd. The steel animal chute was still blocking part of the doorway. Beside it, a few people fell, and more people were pushed down on top of them until the entire way was blocked. People could have escaped through side entrances or under the canvas, but many of them were children—the only way they knew was the way they had come in.

Less than ten minutes after the first flame, the six massive poles of the tent began to buckle and waver. The band members snatched their instruments and ran for safety just as a pole smashed across the stage. The audience members who hadn't found their way out were now caught under the collapsing canvas.

The fire burned itself out in less than 15 minutes, but the largest tent in the world had turned into a black, flame-eaten blanket lying over the bodies of those who hadn't escaped.

Cool Heads in the Furnace

Many who managed to escape the flames owed thanks to a few extraordinarily levelheaded people—people who managed to stay calm while the world around them was exploding into chaos. One of these was a teenager named Donald Anderson. He'd arrived at the circus late, grumbling to himself as he and his grandparents' handyman climbed onto the back bleachers. They'd missed the opening parade, and the seats near the center ring were all taken. Still, he was thrilled as the big cats began to perform. By the time the high-wire act was on, he was craning his neck with the rest of the crowd.

Donald's late arrival would save his life. Just as he heard the emergency announcement, Donald saw a flash of flame and a patch of blue sky open in the top of the tent. Without even stopping to think, he leaped off the top row of the bleachers to the floor below and yanked at the tent canvas. It was tied down.

Donald glanced toward the main entrance. People were already panicking, and he could hear the shouts of children as the crowd pushed and shoved. He shook his head—escape in that direction looked impossible. Then he remembered his pocket knife, tucked into his pants. Within seconds, Donald had sliced a long, thin slit into the tough canvas. Reaching back for the handyman, Donald slid through to safety.

The shrieks inside followed him. There must be some way to help. But even as he poked his head back through the slit with the thought of rescuing others, the heat from inside the tent hit him like a blast from a furnace. He knew it would be deadly to go back. Instead, Donald raced around the perimeter of the tent, cutting more slits in the canvas and yelling at people to come out through the walls. Those who heard him gratefully squeezed through the canvas. Others managed to slide out from beneath the sides of the tent where it wasn't tied down. Soon, crowds of survivors were gathered in the street.

Donald was just one hero in an amazing rescue that combined the efforts of many people. For example, as someone ran through the clown area shouting "Fire!", clown Emmett Kelly looked down and saw the bucket of water that he used to wash off his face paint. He grabbed the bucket and ran outside—still wearing his giant clown shoes—to try to slosh water on the blaze. But the fire was far beyond him. Pouring buckets of water on it was like pouring thimblefuls on a bonfire.

Determined to do something, he ran for the front entrance. There, he found people shoving to get out while others attempted to shove their way back in to find family members.

"You can't get back in there," he yelled. "Keep moving! Keep moving!" And, directed by a clown, survivors staggered across the lot to safety.

Meanwhile, 29-year-old Bill Curlee had also scrambled into action. He'd arrived at the circus with his 8-year-old son and as soon as the trouble started he'd lifted the canvas at the side of the tent and shoved the boy underneath. "Go wait for me by the car," he said.

Having grown up taking care of three younger sisters, Bill knew right away many kids would panic and would need help finding their way out of the crowd. He climbed on top of the steel animal chute near where he had been sitting, and he began lifting children one by one over the metal to safety. He saved dozens of children, but when the canvas roof came crashing down, he found that his leg was trapped in the steel of the cage. He never escaped.

Nearby, Fred Bradna, the man who had blown the circus whistle and alerted everyone to the danger, stood at the front entrance watching in horror as people were trampled in the panic.

"Run for the side flaps," he screamed again and again. No one heard him over the uproar. As his hair caught fire and his skin blistered, Fred began grabbing children, dragging them from the crush of bodies, and shoving them out of the exit. He saved 11 kids before escaping the blaze himself.

When compared to the thousands in the audience, 11 might not have seemed like a large number. But to the 11 children who owed their lives to Fred, he'd achieved something miraculous. And together, Donald, Emmett, Bill, and Fred had managed to save hundreds.

OF COURSE, children weren't the only ones in danger. Outside the big top, the animal handlers known as "bull men" heard the band playing its emergency song and didn't stop to investigate. They called, "Tails! Tails!" At once, the elephants hooked themselves trunk-to-tail and formed a long line. The bull men herded them across the circus lot to safety.

Animal trainer May Kovar felt the heat of the fire on her back—she was still in the chute with the wild cats when the fire erupted. She could easily have run for the end, but instead she stayed and prodded the animals along the metal hallway and back to their cages outside the tent. Thanks to her, the animals lived and children later managed to scramble down the cleared chute and out of the tent.

Picking up the Pieces

As smoke spiraled into the sky and news of the disaster spread, Hartford leaped into action. The Red Cross called in 1500 volunteers. Off-duty hospital staff poured into the local wards, ready to help the wounded. Soon, they were treating more than 480 people, including 60 circus employees, for burns and smoke inhalation.

At the State Guard Armory, ambulances delivered body after body and workers laid them side by side on cots. More than half the bodies were children, and almost all the rest were women. Thousands had escaped, but a total of 168 people lay dead, unrecognizable after the flames.

In the armory and the hospital hallways, fathers who just an hour ago had been peacefully working, unaware of the fire, found themselves scanning the crowd and wondering if their loved ones were still alive. Fortunately, most of the mothers and children who had been separated during the flames managed to escape and later find each other.

In the end, six people remained unidentified—probably those whose entire families were lost in the blaze. The youngest mystery body was that of a small girl who became known as Little Miss 1565, remembered by the number assigned to her at the morgue. According to the local legend that sprang up, she and her mother were killed in the fire on the same day as her father was killed in the fighting of World War II.

As funeral processions were winding through the city (funerals were being held every 15 minutes at some funeral homes), police cars were scooping up the leaders of the circus and charging them with manslaughter. At the same time, lawyers for the families of the dead children began to sue.

It was the worst circus fire in history, and the company could easily have declared bankruptcy. Its liability insurance only covered $500,000, and it was obvious that millions of dollars in lawsuits would have to be paid. But the entire Ringling family agreed that they should work to repay the families as much as possible. The next summer, they staged the circus without a tent, using stadiums and baseball parks, and began to settle the lawsuits. Over the next several years, they earned $5,000,000 for the families of those killed in the fire. Most of the circus leaders served short jail sentences.

No one knows for sure what started the fire. A 21-year-old circus worker told a reporter that he had done it, but the man had a history of mental problems and police could never decide whether he was telling the truth. In the end, many people agreed with the clown, Emmett Kelly, who told reporters that everyone should put the fire out of their minds as soon as possible.

"We must entertain," he said. "In wartime, it's more important than ever."

Led by dedicated performers like Emmett, the show continued. Today, it remains the largest and most successful American circus.

Introduction

Krieger, Michael. *All the Men in the Sea.* New York: The Free Press, 2002.

"Yarri—A Frontier Story." From the Australian Broadcasting Corporation website. www.abc.net.au/lateline/content/2003/hc16. htm

Death on the North Face

Anker, Daniel, ed. *Eiger: The Vertical Arena.* Seattle: The Mountaineers Books, 2000.

Harrer, Heinrich. *The White Spider.* London: Paladin Grafton Books, 1989.

Olsen, Jack. *The Climb Up to Hell.* New York: St. Martin's Griffin, 1998.

Roth, Arthur. *Eiger: Wall of Death.* New York: W.W. Norton & Company, 1982.

Hope in the Storm

Calvert, Rev. R. *The Story of Abigail Becker.* Toronto: William Briggs, 1899.

Cardiff, John. "The Heroine of Long Point." From the Norfolk Heritage Center website. www.norfolklore.com

Wittier, J.G. "The Heroine of Long Point." *Atlantic Monthly.* May 1869.

The Mountain That Walked

Anderson, Frank. *The Frank Slide Story*. Frontier Books, 1968.

Bergman, Brian. "The Day the Mountain Moved." *Maclean's*. April 28, 2003. p. 58.

"Earthquake Rockslide Overwhelms Frank, N.W.T." *The Globe*. April 30, 1903. p.1.

Finlayson, David. "If Turtle Mountain Moves, We'll Have Advance Warning." *Edmonton Journal*. June 8, 2005. p. G1.

Frank Slide 100th Anniversary Commemorative Booklet. Frank, Alberta: Frank Slide Interpretive Centre, 2003.

Nantel, Hon W.B., A.P. Low, and R.W. Black. *Report of the Commission Appointed to Investigate Turtle Mountain, Frank, Alberta, 1911*. Ottawa, Government Printing Bureau, 1912.

Operation Gwamba

Walsh, John and Robert Gannon. *Time Is Short and the Water Rises*. New York: E.P. Dutton & Co., 1967.

Wayman, Stan. "'Operation Gwamba' to Rescue the Animals." *Life*. January 22, 1965. pp. 24–29.

World Society for the Protection of Animals website. www.wspa-international.org

Alone in the Arctic

Cross, Wilbur. *Disaster at the Pole*. New York: The Lyons Press, 2000.

Hogg, Garry. *Airship over the Pole*. London: Abelard-Schuman, 1969.

Deadline for Death

"4 Days of Fear, Then 7 Minutes for the Daring Rescue in Mogadishu." *New York Times*. October 19, 1977. pp. 15–16.

Tanner, Henry. "German Troops Free Hostages on Hijacked Plane in Somalia; At Least 3 Terrorists Killed." *New York Times*. October 18, 1977. pp. A1, 12.

"The New War on Terrorism." *Newsweek*. October 31, 1977. pp. 48–56.

Five Dark Days

Lewis, Barbara A. *Kids with Courage*. Minneapolis: Free Spirit Publishing, 1992.

Proctor, Maurine Jensen. "Lost in a Mine." *Meridian*. November 1, 2001.

Roche, Lisa Riley. "Alive." *Deseret News*. September 28, 1989. p. A1.

Spangler, Jerry. "Hope Fading Fast for Boy Lost 4 Days. Searchers Now Battling Fatigue, Despair." *Deseret News*. September 26, 1989. p. B1.

Undercover Hero

Barker, Greg, producer. *Ghosts of Rwanda*. Video. PBS, 2004.

Doyle, Mark. "Captain Mbaye Diagne." *Granta*. Summer 1994. pp. 98–103.

Pugliese, David. "Dallaire's Mission." *The Ottawa Citizen*. September 22, 2002. p. C1.

Entombed Underwater

Dunmore, Spencer. *Lost Subs*. Toronto: Madison Press Books, 2002.

Maas, Peter. *The Terrible Hours*. New York: Perennial, 2001.

"Statement of Harold C. Preble, Naval Architect, USS *Squalus* Survivor." Naval Historical Center website. www.history.navy.mil/fags/fag99-6.html

"USS *Squalus* (SS-192): Lecture by Charles Momsen on Rescue and Salvage." Naval Historical Center website. www.history.navy.mil/fags/fag99-6.html

Chaos under the Big Top

Culhane, John. *The American Circus*. New York: Henry Holt & Company, 1990.

"Death Stops a Circus." *Newsweek*. July 17, 1944. pp. 31–32.

Goode, Steven. "Hundreds Dedicate Circus Fire Memorial." *Hartford Courant*. July 7, 2005.

Karmel, Terese. "Hero with a pocket knife recalls circus fire." *Chronicle*. August 7, 1997. p. B3.

North, Henry Ringling and Alden Hatch. *The Circus Kings*. New York: Doubleday & Company, 1960.

"Six Minutes." *Time*. July 17, 1944. pp. 3–4.

Index

About the Author

Tanya Lloyd Kyi was once trapped in an emergency shelter for two days during a winter storm, and has no desire ever to go near the pack ice of the north pole. When she is not researching rescue stories, she is warm and dry in her Vancouver home with her husband and daughter. Tanya is the author of eight books, including *Fires!*, *The Blue Jean Book*, and *Jared Lester: Fifth Grade Jester*.